The *DeShaney* Case

LANDMARK LAW CASES

&

AMERICAN SOCIETY

Peter Charles Hoffer
N. E. H. Hull
Series Editors

For a complete list of titles in the series go to www.kansaspress.ku.edu

LYNNE CURRY

The *DeShaney* Case

Child Abuse, Family Rights, and the Dilemma of State Intervention

UNIVERSITY PRESS OF KANSAS

Published by the University Press of Kansas (Lawrence, Kansas 66045), which was organized by the Kansas Board of Regents and is operated and funded by Emporia State University, Fort Hays State University, Kansas State University, Pittsburg State University, the University of Kansas, and Wichita State University

Library of Congress Cataloging-in-Publication Data

Curry, Lynne.

The DeShaney case : child abuse, family rights, and the dilemma of
state intervention / Lynne Curry.

p. cm. — (Landmark law cases & American society)

Includes bibliographical references and index.

ISBN-13: 978-0-7006-1496-7 (cloth : alk. paper)

ISBN-13: 978-0-7006-1497-4 (pbk. : alk. paper)

1. DeShaney, Melody—Trials, litigation, etc.   2. Winnebago County
(Wis.). Dept. of Social Services—Trials, litigation, etc.   3. DeShaney,
Joshua, 1979–   4. Child abuse—Law and legislation—United States.   5.
Due process of law—United States.   1. Winnebago County (Wis.). Dept. of
Social Services.   11. Title.

KF228.D464C87   2007

345.73′025554—dc22

2006034359

British Library Cataloguing-in-Publication Data is available.

Printed in the United States of America

10 9 8 7 6 5 4 3 2 1

For Brandon, Ian, and Sam

CONTENTS

One of the most common, shocking, and yet often hidden tragedies in our society is the abuse of children by their caregivers. We learn of these cases when they come to the law, and since the widespread recognition of the signals of the battered child syndrome, state and local agencies have exercised their power to inquire, inspect, and even remove a child from an abusive household. But like the introduction of compulsory primary and secondary school education in the nineteenth century, the intrusion of child welfare agencies into the domestic setting has become a subject of controversy. For underfunded, insufficiently trained, and overworked agencies can miss even obvious cases, or fail to act with adequate speed and decisiveness.

Such was the case with Wisconsin's Joshua DeShaney, repeatedly beaten by his father, Randy, from 1979 to 1984. Joshua's injuries were catastrophic, in large measure because the state did not remove him from the care of his father despite his caseworker and emergency room personnel recognizing all the signs of abuse. The state had a comprehensive system that left the child's safety in the hands of social workers, one of whom had to act to rescue the child. If the state, through Winnebago County's child care services, did not act, then who was to protect the child from his own parent?

Suit was brought in federal court by the noncustodial parent, Melody, against the state for failing in its own duties. The state vigorously defended itself, arguing that it was not at fault. The culprit, Joshua's father, had already been tried and found guilty by a lower court. Were the state to be held financially liable for the failings of its agencies, then it might also have to pay if the fire service failed to save a victim or the police departments did not prevent a crime.

The case ultimately wound up before the U.S. Supreme Court. A divided Court rendered a controversial decision, with far-reaching consequences. Critics and supporters weighed in, for at stake were the concepts of the primacy of the family, the duty of the state to protect all its citizens, and the role of law in the most intimate of all social relationships. *DeShaney v. Winnebago County*, a case in which the plaintiff was the weakest member of society, raised fundamental questions. As Lynne Curry astutely explains, the case went to the very heart of constitutional jurisprudence — was the U.S. Constitution a positive document creating a mutually supportive community, or was it, in the words of Judge Richard Posner, "a charter of negative liberties," allowing the state to intervene or not, as it chose, and immunizing it from its own failings?

Curry's fast-paced and insightful tale is one we cannot put down, nor should we. She has opened the records of the state, peering inside its legal machinery, interviewed the principals in the case, empathized with their pain and suffering, and still kept an appropriate scholarly distance. Using materials from Randy DeShaney's criminal trial, she has recovered the shocking story that led to the case. She then follows the suit through the federal courts to the highest tribunal. Her analysis of the majority and dissenting opinions is a marvel of clarity. But she does not stop here, for the implications of the decision reached out into the public debate and influenced child protective standards throughout the country.

ACKNOWLEDGMENTS

I am very grateful to have had the support of many institutions and individuals while I worked on this project. A summer stipend awarded by the National Endowment for the Humanities in 2005 supported the completion of my research and enabled me to work full time on writing the manuscript. Any views, findings, conclusions, or recommendations expressed in this publication do not necessarily reflect those of the National Endowment for the Humanities. Eastern Illinois University has been extremely generous, supporting my research in 2004 with a summer research award granted by the Council on Faculty Research. The College of Arts and Humanities funded conference travel as well as stipends for graduate research assistants. I wish to thank especially Dean James Johnson of the college for his support as well as former graduate assistants Annie Tock and Mary Barford for their able and enthusiastic help. Matthew Berry went above and beyond the call of duty in locating individuals, keeping track of details, and accompanying me to dig through the archives. My colleagues in the History Department have buoyed my spirits by their continued interest in the project, and I would like to acknowledge especially Debra Reid and Martin J. Hardeman in this regard. Finally, I am grateful to Northwestern University's Department of History and the Weinberg College of Arts and Sciences for supporting my initial undertakings in this project during the period from 2001 to 2003 while I was a visiting faculty member there.

When working on a book project, one accumulates a great many debts to people who provide advice and assistance along the way. I have benefited greatly from the generosity of numerous individuals, as the bibliographic essay included at the end of this volume demonstrates. Here I would like to thank the professional staffs at the Library of Congress Manuscripts Division, Wisconsin Historical Society, University of Illinois at Urbana-Champaign College of Law Library, Booth Library at Eastern Illinois University, National Archives and Records Administration (Great Lakes Region), Everett McKinley Dirksen U.S. Courthouse, Office of the Clerk of Courts at the Winnebago County Courthouse, Records Division of the Oshkosh Police Department, and the Wisconsin Department of Justice Crime Information Bureau. My appreciation also goes to Edward Foley, Tinsley E. Yarbrough, Mark J. Mingo, Keith Nelson, Cynthia Bowman, Travis McDade, Diane Fremgen, and Jerry Goldman for answering my questions and pointing me in the right direction. I owe a very special debt to Donald Sullivan, Curry First, Michael Novotny, Christopher Hansen, and William Glaberson for the invaluable insights they provided into the case.

Several people have read and provided comments on draft versions of the chapters presented in this volume. I am especially grateful to the scholars who attended the conference "Raising Americans, Raising Europeans in the Twentieth Century," sponsored by the German Historical Institute in Washington, D.C., in spring 2005, who gave my work their careful attention and critiques. Their insights have enabled me to begin thinking about the story I have pieced together within an international context. I would like to acknowledge especially Dirk Schumann, Sonya Michel, Seth Koven, and Katherine Bullard. My heartfelt thanks also go to Sonya Michel and to Christopher R. Waldrep for their willingness, over many years, to read and guide my work and to continue to fill the role of scholarly mentors. Of course, any errors of fact or interpretation in this book are entirely my own responsibility.

The genesis of this project was a pleasant and stimulating discussion I had with Michael Briggs, editor in chief of the University Press of Kansas. The book would not have come into being without his continued interest, wisdom, and patience, for which I am deeply appreciative. My thanks also go to Fred M. Woodward, director of the press, and to the editorial staff, whose professional skills and hard work transformed a manuscript into a book. Certainly not least, I would like to thank the editors of the series Landmark Law Cases and American Society, N. E. H. Hull and Peter Charles Hoffer, for allowing me to make what I hope will be a useful contribution to their wonderful series.

As always, my deepest debt is to my family, which remains my most important source of support and inspiration. I am, more than ever, grateful for their love and support.

Introduction

In February 1989, the U.S. Supreme Court handed down its decision in *DeShaney v. Winnebago County Department of Social Services.* The opinion, written by Chief Justice William Rehnquist writing for a six-to-three majority, attracted considerable public attention, for it involved the sad and troubling issue of child abuse. The chief justice began his opinion by noting that "the facts of this case are undeniably tragic." Joshua DeShaney, a four-year-old child living in central Wisconsin, had been severely beaten by his father and legal custodian, Randy DeShaney, leaving the little boy severely brain damaged and partially paralyzed. The troubled DeShaney household was well known to the caseworkers at the Winnebago County Department of Social Services, who had first received reports of the abuse some eighteen months earlier; a child protective worker from the department, in fact, had been supervising the family for more than a year. During that time, Joshua had been seen on numerous occasions by emergency room personnel at two different local hospitals as well as by police officers in two Winnebago County cities. The caseworker had made several notes in her files referring to her suspicions about the boy's frequent injuries, which were always explained away as "accidents" by the adults in the household. The state had taken temporary custody of Joshua on one occasion when he was brought to the hospital with a suspicious head injury and the medical staff observed extensive bruising on the child's body while they prepared him to be x-rayed. But the child was returned to his father's home the following day. Several months later he was brought to the hospital again, this time in a coma. Emergency neurosurgery performed on the boy revealed medical evidence that he had sustained several previous brain injuries, apparently occurring over a period of time.

Family violence was very much on the public's mind in the winter of 1989. A great deal of media attention had surrounded another horrific instance of child abuse, this one occurring in New York City. Six-year-old Elizabeth ("Lisa") Steinberg had been severely beaten and shockingly neglected by her adoptive parents. Joel Steinberg was convicted of first degree manslaughter in a trial that began in October 1988 and kept the public riveted for more than three months as people followed the case intently on television and in the print media. Televised trials were relatively new in 1988, undoubtedly accounting for much of the public's heightened interest. But the extensive attention paid to this case also arose in part because the perpetrators, Joel Steinberg and Hedda Nussbaum, were perceived by many Americans as atypical of the kinds of parents who abuse their children. Contrary to stereotypical images, this family did not belong to a racial minority, was not poverty stricken, and did not live in a housing project in a dangerous area of the city. Rather, Steinberg and Nussbaum were a white, well-educated, professional couple. Steinberg was a criminal attorney, and Nussbaum (who also suffered physical and psychological abuse from Steinberg) was a former editor of children's books at Random House. The couple lived in Manhattan's West Village in an expensive apartment in a brownstone building that reportedly was once Mark Twain's home. As family law scholar Martha Minow has observed, the couple's egregious behavior had prompted the millions of Americans who followed the media coverage of Lisa Steinberg's terrible death to ask themselves, "who could believe that such people could act like that?" And yet, plenty of people had believed, for the extensive publicity about the case revealed that numerous individuals coming in contact with the family had made their concerns for Lisa's safety known to authorities. Eventually Lisa's birth mother, an unmarried college student at the time of the girl's birth, successfully sued the city of New York for its failure to protect Lisa.

The Supreme Court's opinion in *DeShaney v. Winnebago County* was handed down just two weeks after Joel Steinberg's well-publicized conviction. Although not as sensationalized as the Steinberg criminal trial, the case did receive substantial attention in the press as well as among legal scholars. Concerned citizens wrote letters to newspapers — and to the justices themselves — both supporting and vilifying the decision. During the months preceding oral arguments, presented in November 1988, and for weeks after the Court handed down its ruling three months later, the public learned of Joshua's repeated beatings at the hands of his father, the apparent awareness on the part of social service workers that the little boy was in trouble, and the state's failure to protect him, with devastating consequences. It was a shocking and distressing story. By the time the opinion was rendered, Randy DeShaney had already served time in a Wisconsin prison for felony child abuse. Thus the public could be assured that the perpetrator had been brought to justice for what happened to Joshua. But, like the sad story of Lisa Steinberg, the case from America's heartland raised another, larger question that continued to haunt the public: Why wasn't this tragedy prevented?

Joshua's fate came before the nine justices of the Supreme Court in the form of a civil lawsuit filed by the child and his mother, Melody DeShaney, against the State of Wisconsin's Department of Social Services. (Melody DeShaney, who lived in Wyoming, had surrendered legal custody of Joshua to his father shortly after the couple had divorced years earlier.) The suit asked the Supreme Court to consider whether the agency's failure to protect Joshua from his father's beatings violated the child's constitutional rights under the Fourteenth Amendment. Ratified in 1868, the amendment protects citizens' rights to life, liberty, and property against infringement by the states without due process of the law. Ever since, federal courts have interpreted the boundaries of the states' liability under the Fourteenth Amendment in thousands of cases asking the same basic question: Precisely what actions taken by a state constitute a violation of the due process clause?

Joshua's case asked the Supreme Court to consider a broad definition of "state action." The State of Wisconsin, the plaintiffs asserted, had erected a child protective system that endowed social workers with exclusive power to remove children from violent homes (under Wisconsin law, police did not have this power). But, despite considerable evidence that Joshua was being abused by his father, they charged, state social service workers had failed to take appropriate action, resulting in violations of the child's constitutional rights to life and liberty. For the plaintiffs, the "state action" in Joshua's case consisted of Wisconsin (1) setting up a child protective system that rendered the child completely dependent on social workers to rescue him, (2) initiating his rescue through a caseworker's extensive involvement with the family, and (3) ultimately failing to employ its own system to save Joshua DeShaney from terrible, permanent harm. Although not unprecedented in the area of civil rights law, an expansive reading of "state action" as it pertained to the provision of social services remained rather new in the 1980s and was still under development in several cases then making their way through the federal courts, several of which concerned abused children and the failure of state child protective services to save them from grievous injury or death. Thus the Court's decision in the *DeShaney* case would have possible ramifications not only for Joshua and other victims of domestic violence but also for those who were seeking constitutional claims to the states' provisions of social services such as police protection and emergency medical assistance.

The defendant, the Winnebago County Department of Social Services, countered that the definition of "state action" the plaintiffs sought from the Supreme Court was overly broad — even dangerously so. They argued that Joshua and his mother could not claim a constitutional violation occurred because no actions taken by the state had actually caused the harm to the boy. The beatings, they pointed out, had been administered by Randy DeShaney, a private actor. The Fourteenth Amendment's protections for citizens' rights refer exclusively to infringements by the state; they do not safeguard individuals from privately inflicted harm. The defendants further argued that a ruling for Joshua would place constitutional liability on all state-sponsored social services, thereby placing states' ability to provide them in jeopardy. A virtual "floodgate" of possible lawsuits would result if the Court found in favor of Joshua, they warned. Would firefighters be held liable for failing to put out a fire before it destroyed a citizen's home? Would police officers be liable for failing to prevent a barroom brawl that resulted in the death of a patron? Litigating these thorny cases, the defendants asserted, would bankrupt states and force them to cease offering vital services to the public.

In seeking Fourteenth Amendment protections for Joshua, *DeShaney v. Winnebago County* raised the profound issue of whether children are endowed with rights independent of those of their parents. Coming before the Court in the late 1980s, the case followed several decades of liberal constitutional jurisprudence that expanded the universe of civil rights to encompass protections against discrimination on the bases of race, ethnicity, and gender; some scholars have referred to a "children's liberation" movement that developed in the path of this trajectory. But to say children have *rights* — as opposed to having "needs" or "interests" — is no simple statement in law, for civil rights empower individuals in very particular, concrete ways.

To claim something as a right necessarily obligates others, including the state, to respect and protect it. But, of course, children do not exist in society as empowered, independent beings; they are inherently dependent on adults. Anglo-American common law, in fact, has for centuries recognized and protected the rights not of children but rather of their parents — particularly their fathers — to raise their offspring in the way they see fit, free from intrusion by the state. The underlying assumption of this long legal tradition has been that children will be best served when the law protects their parents' liberties.

Some legal scholars have argued that the legal paradigm historically governing the family is actually akin to the structure regulating private property, and as such it has not always functioned in the interests of children themselves. By tradition, the law assigned children a status resembling that of chattel, or personal property, belonging to their fathers. Fathers enjoyed a range of vested rights in their children, including the right to use their offsprings' labor (or hire it out for others to put into service), transfer their guardianship to others, and employ physical punishment in order to discipline and control them. Courts long recognized a right of compensation to fathers should the actions of others cause them to lose their vested rights in their children. In 1870, for example, the Illinois Supreme Court in *O'Connell v. Turner* curbed that state's power to commit juveniles who had committed no crimes to state reform schools. Although the court did assert due process rights for children (noting that the "disability" of being minors did not "make slaves or criminals" of them), it also construed the Illinois reform school law to be contrary to the rights of parents, who had the "right to the care, custody, and assistance" of their children. Further, the court affirmed parental power over children as "an emanation from God" with the consequence that "every attempt to infringe upon it, except from dire necessity, should be resisted in all well-governed States." State interference with the private family, in other words, threatened to disrupt the entire social order. Similarly, in the 1918 decision *Hammer v.*

Dagenhart, the U.S. Supreme Court struck down a federal law prohibiting child labor, in part because it interfered with fathers' rights to their children's earnings.

The foundational Supreme Court opinions safeguarding parental rights in modern U.S. constitutional law are *Meyer v. Nebraska* (1923) and *Pierce v. Society of Sisters* (1925), two opinions that legal scholar Barbara Bennett Woodhouse has dubbed "liberal icons" usually cited as landmark victories for the protection of religious liberty and intellectual freedom. In *Meyer*, the Court overturned a Nebraska statute that prohibited the teaching of German in public schools, a language spoken by the inhabitants of a rural community who wanted their children to maintain the customs and traditions of their forebears. Justice James C. McReynolds's opinion charged the state legislature with "attempting to interfere . . . with the power of parents to control the education of their own." Two years later, Justice McReynolds built upon his ruling in *Meyer* by striking down an Oregon statute requiring parents to send their children to public, rather than private or parochial, primary schools. "We think it entirely plain," the justice wrote, "that the [Oregon law] unreasonably interferes with the liberty of parents and guardians to direct the upbringing and education of children under their control." Although the Court's steadfast promotion of parents' liberties regarding their children is apparent, it is also noteworthy that the opinion employs the particular phrases "their own" and "under their control." As Woodhouse has argued, these opinions are actually firmly rooted in traditional views about parents' ownership of their children and, as a consequence, have served to embed within modern family law the notion that children are not individuals per se but rather are conduits of their parents' identities, values, and aspirations. Granting independent rights to children raises the specter that they will exercise them not only in their own interests, but possibly against the rights and interests of adults, with destructive consequences for the family and the proper ordering of society. Four-year-old Joshua's claim before the Supreme Court for constitutional rights of his own, therefore, challenged long-standing legal, social, and cultural constructions of the family as well as deep-seated beliefs about the appropriate role of the state in relation to the private household.

State-sponsored child welfare services in the United States are integrally tied to the role of the legal system in seeking to preserve the private family. Although organized interventions to protect victims of domestic violence date to the nineteenth century, the child protection system that encountered, and ultimately failed, Joshua DeShaney was a product of the post–World War II period. Beginning in the 1960s and 1970s, social service providers made a near-universal commitment to the "family preservation model" as the acceptable professional framework for their interventions in troubled households. The family preservation model was the product of considerable political pressure on states to reduce the number of children in the foster care system, which had ballooned after World War II, at ever-rising public expense and, as many child welfare experts warned, to the great detriment of the children themselves. Under this model, caseworkers served as intermediaries between their clients and the network of social services provided by the states. Significantly, under the family preservation model caseworkers undertook responsibility for all members of the household rather than the children exclusively. Thus the professionals who acted as "child protective workers" in a state's social service apparatus in actuality played dual roles. In one role they were the "healer" of the family unit, teaching parenting skills, for example, or enrolling their clients in state-sponsored activities and assistance programs. It was a role that required a helpful, therapeutic orientation toward the family. In order for the model to be employed successfully, caseworkers must invest considerable time and attention in gaining the trust and cooperation of their clients.

Conversely, however, child protective workers also embodied the state's authority to remove children from their parents' homes when they deemed it necessary to do so. In the 1980s Wisconsin, like most states, gave the power to determine that necessity to social workers rather than to police officers or other law enforcement agents; although the actual orders for removal were issued by a family court judge, the initiative to begin the proceedings was assigned to social service departments. All reports of suspected child abuse, both voluntary and mandatory (those required by law of teachers or medical personnel, for example), were routed to the child protective worker assigned to the family involved, who in turn made decisions about what, if any, actions should be taken. Thus an enormous amount of responsibility for safeguarding children rested on the professional judgment of caseworkers, and the state required them to take an authoritative, even punitive, approach toward their clients in order to carry out their role as the protectors of children. The family preservation model, therefore, necessitated that the family caseworker make a crucial professional judgment about when to switch roles, from one that was basically therapeutic and cooperative, working with family members to help them access social services and assuage their difficulties, to one that was fundamentally authoritative and punitive, judging parents to be unfit and removing children from their custody temporarily or perhaps permanently. It was a shift that the caseworker who took on the responsibility of shoring up the troubled DeShaney household failed to make, with dire consequences for Joshua. A close investigation of the events leading to Joshua DeShaney's tragic fate exposes the weaknesses of this widely adopted system for protecting children living in violent homes.

But many child welfare advocates urge us to be cautious in giving up on the family preservation model. As legal scholar Dorothy E. Roberts has pointed out, public criticisms of the system are often motivated as much by political struggles over race and class as by concern for the welfare of children. In 1997, Congress passed the Adoption and Safe Families Act, which aimed at increasing the number of foster-care children available for adoption by limiting the time allowed for reconciliation with their families. The nature of the debate surrounding the act, Roberts has argued, revealed the extent to which race and class politics drove overzealous calls for "children's rights," a form of public pressure that artificially and destructively pitted children against their biological families. "Children's rights," Roberts cautions, can be employed as a political slogan for blaming disadvantaged parents and avoiding the social investment of adequate resources into poor and minority families and communities.

This book offers an examination of *DeShaney v. Winnebago County* from a historical perspective. It reconstructs several interrelated contexts in which the case was originated, adjudicated, and resolved, including the historical development of child protection services, the evolution of the crime of child abuse, and the trajectory of Fourteenth Amendment jurisprudence. In the process, it reveals a number of essential — and disturbing — themes that reflect U.S. society in the late twentieth century and continue to shape our society today. Among these are Americans' attitudes toward and beliefs about the family and domestic relations; the causes and nature of child abuse and the appropriate remedies for abolishing it; and the proper functions, responsibilities, and limits of the state in intervening in citizens' private lives. As individuals we are rightfully shocked by revelations about the physical abuse and neglect of children, and we find ourselves moved to decry their occurrence. But as a society we are considerably less certain about the hard choices we must make as we weigh the costs and benefits involved in order to make meaningful efforts to alleviate the problem.

Although *DeShaney v. Winnebago County* has garnered a great deal of attention from legal scholars over the years, its significance for the larger picture of modern U.S. history has received less consideration to date. Like all landmark law cases, the tragic story of Joshua DeShaney offers us a way to learn something about the past that extends beyond the analytical confines of court procedures and legal briefs — artifacts that, although extremely instructive, can often seem dry or impenetrable to the layperson. A historical analysis of *DeShaney v. Winnebago County* offers an unusual opportunity to examine closely the complex workings of a state social service bureaucracy as well as the various permutations of the legal pathways taken by the criminal case against Randy DeShaney and the civil suit that came before the nation's High Court. Further, as we gain a new understanding of the past, we may come to learn something about ourselves as well. It is my hope, therefore, that the interpretation I offer here will begin to rectify the existing gap in historical scholarship on *DeShaney v. Winnebago County*.

Americans have a profoundly ambivalent view of the role that the state should play in our daily lives. We cherish our privacy and closely guard it from intrusion by government entities. Many conservative jurists point to the U.S. Constitution as a "charter of negative liberties," in the words of Federal Appeals Court Judge Richard Posner, who authored the Seventh Circuit's opinion in Joshua's case. The Constitution, this view holds, is designed to ensure individual freedom by limiting the actions of the state. On the one hand, the family is regarded as the most sacrosanct of all private social institutions, and decades of legal and constitutional evolution have supported this basic tenet. On the other hand, history also demonstrates that our society is constructed so that not all citizens are equally capable of achieving self-reliance. Therefore civil rights law has developed — after 1868, but most notably in the latter half of the twentieth century — to reflect the various vulnerabilities of different categories of individuals and to employ the power of the state in order to ensure their liberties. Children, particularly those living in violent and abusive households, are the most vulnerable of all citizens. They are physically, financially, psychologically, and legally dependent on their parents, guardians, teachers, physicians, and many other adults for their very survival. When adults fail children in egregious ways — when, in the words of Joshua's counsel, the "child's protector becomes the predator" — these dependents have only the assurance of an active, vigilant state to protect their lives. The state may punish the perpetrators of child abuse, just as Joel Steinberg and Randy DeShaney were duly punished, with terms in prison. But, we continue to ask ourselves, could the state do more to prevent these tragedies from happening in the first place? Should it do so?

History is a humanistic discipline, and one of the advantages of writing legal history is the opportunity to put human faces on the cases that have made their way through the courts and in so doing have served to shape our own time. The compelling story of Joshua DeShaney is a particularly moving example. In relating the story of *DeShaney v. Winnebago County* I believe it important not to lose sight of the fact that, at the very heart of a Supreme Court case in which major constitutional questions were debated and decided, there remained a small child whose very fate depended on the outcome. As a historian, I have utilized not only the legal briefs and opinions the case engendered but also a range of other sources including social work case files, medical testimony, legal depositions, police reports, media coverage, and oral histories with the twin goals of constructing a more complete narrative of Joshua's story and illuminating the wider contexts in which the case unfolded. Wisconsin is an "open-records state," and thus a great many materials I sought in order to flesh out the narrative were made readily available to me. I also had the great fortune to interview a number of individuals who were willing to discuss their experiences and provide me with their own perspectives on the case. Along with such opportunities, however, also came a high degree of responsibility, for the story I have endeavored to tell involved a great deal of pain, grief, and disappointment for the actors involved — sensitivities and emotions not consigned solely to the past, but continuing to affect their lives today. Not all the individuals I contacted were able or willing to discuss their involvement with the case, and in those instances I have attempted to represent their experiences and views as faithfully as I can using the other sources available to me.

This book is about child abuse, a topic with dimensions that are both profoundly public and deeply private. In writing about *DeShaney v. Winnebago County*, I have been constantly aware that a fine line exists between providing information pertinent to furthering readers' understanding of the case and avoiding a voyeuristic invasion of the private lives of people who are still living as this volume goes to publication. Significantly, the arguments Joshua's counsel presented in the courts depended heavily on the fact that he was abused severely and repeatedly over a period of time, rather than during one particularly violent episode. Conveying the exact nature of his injuries therefore was quite material to the case and was extensively detailed in depositions from medical personnel. Much of this information was also introduced in Randy DeShaney's criminal trial, where it became part of the public record in Wisconsin. I have made a good faith effort to convey pertinent information that enlightens the reader about the case and aids in understanding its meaning for the larger historical picture. At the same time, I have deliberately avoided the inclusion of other material that, although publicly available to any researcher, I have judged to be extraneous to my narrative and unnecessarily invasive to certain individuals' privacy.

Chapter One details Joshua's story from his birth in 1979 to his final beating March 8, 1984, just two weeks short of his fifth birthday. Chapter Two traces child protection services as they developed in the United States during the nineteenth and twentieth centuries. Chapter Three focuses on Randy DeShaney's criminal trial and the legal and social evolution of child abuse as a punishable crime rather than a regrettable fact of family life. Chapter Four examines the civil suit *DeShaney v. Winnebago County* as it originated in the federal district court in Wisconsin, the legal arguments presented, and the ways in which the suit was shaped by Judge John W. Reynolds's handling of the case. Chapter Five follows Joshua's case to the U.S. Court of Appeals for the Seventh Circuit and its subsequent appeal to the U.S. Supreme Court, including the oral arguments before the nine justices, and finally Chief Justice Rehnquist's opinion in the case. Chapter Six considers the dissenting opinions written by Justices William Brennan and Harry Blackmun, the public's reaction to the opinions, and discussion of the case in the press and legal scholarship. Finally, the chapter considers the impact of the case on civil rights jurisprudence, child protective work, and the individuals whose lives were changed by the events surrounding Joshua's story.

Joshua's Story

By the time he came to the attention of the Winnebago County Department of Social Services (DSS) in January 1983, three-year-old Joshua had already seen a world of trouble. A photograph of the child published in *Time* magazine in 1989, the year his case was decided by the U.S. Supreme Court, shows a thin, wiry-looking boy holding a kitten. He is dressed in a sleeveless "muscle" shirt and his skinny arms appear tanned from long hours playing outdoors. His face is markedly triangular, with small, sharp features, and his sandy hair, with bangs cut straight across his forehead, looks bleached by the sun. He is looking directly into the camera with a slight but decidedly impish smile, and one senses neither he nor the kitten remained still for very long after the photo was taken. One observer described him as looking "like a regular kid."

Joshua Eli DeShaney was born in Cheyenne, Wyoming, on March 21, 1979, to a young couple, Melody and Randy DeShaney. Randy DeShaney had joined the U.S. Air Force directly after graduating from high school in 1976, serving four years before receiving an honorable discharge. The marriage was both troubled and short-lived, and the couple divorced in 1980. Randy, a brown-haired, blue-eyed man who has been described as both "open" and "quick to anger" by those who knew him, left Melody and the infant Joshua to return to central Wisconsin, where his extended family of siblings and half-siblings resided. His parents also lived in Wisconsin, although they had been divorced when Randy was just six months old; Randy's father, Tom DeShaney, a trucker who lived near Stevens Point, had subsequently remarried and divorced twice. Randy soon remarried as well. He had received a knee injury in the Air Force and upon returning to Wisconsin found that it required surgery. As a result, he had a difficult time holding down a job.

When Joshua was fourteen months old, Melody told her mother, Myrna Bridgewater, that she no longer could take care of him. She was twenty-one and living an unsettled life in Phoenix, Arizona. She agreed to surrender custody of the boy to Randy and his new wife Christine, who were living in Neenah, Wisconsin, a small town on the shores of Lake Winnebago that promotes itself as "a friendly, spirited 'hometown,' where life is safe, comfortable, and secure." In a 1989 interview with William Glaberson of the *New York Times*, Melody recalled thinking that Joshua would have a "nice kid life" living with two parents among extended family in small-town Wisconsin, a life she felt she herself was "too young, too alone, and too poor" to give him.

Melody is often described as a pretty woman. Photographs display abundant dark hair, dark eyes, and a long narrow face with delicate features much like Joshua's. But she had problems in 1980. The divorce had been acrimonious. There were allegations that she had been unfaithful to Randy as well as an unfit mother. When Randy agreed to take custody of his son, he initially wanted to deny Melody visitation rights, but Melody refused to sign the decree. In December 1980, after the decree was modified to allow her to visit her son, Melody returned to Cheyenne and signed the official paperwork. Later the same day she took the toddler to her mother's home, where Christine and Randy's brother Kim had arranged to pick him up the following morning. Randy could not make the trip himself because he was in the hospital recovering from a staph infection he had contracted following the knee surgery. Melody later recalled staying for a few hours at her mother's house, and then she left Joshua. Christine and Kim later claimed that when they picked up Joshua at the Bridgewater house, his bottle had been laced with liquor, a charge Melody vigorously denied. They also believed that Joshua had been underfed.

Shortly after returning to Phoenix, Melody embarked on a two-month road trip with her new boyfriend, a trucker named Swede. Her life became peripatetic. Nevertheless, she made monthly child support payments of $150, sending the checks not to her former husband's home address, which she didn't know, but rather via the Laramie County clerk's office in Cheyenne. She did not speak to nor see her son for more than two years, although she later insisted that she had made between twenty and thirty attempts, only to be "stonewalled" by one of Randy's many relatives on each occasion. For news about Joshua she depended on her mother, who remained in contact with Randy and Christine for awhile and made a few visits to see her grandson in Neenah. Although Melody had no direct knowledge of Joshua's new life, she believed there was no particular reason to suspect anything was wrong. But the next time Melody saw her son, more than two years later, he was severely brain damaged and partially paralyzed, the end result of many months of physical abuse.

Clearly, Randy's home had not provided the "nice kid life" Melody had envisioned for Joshua. Randy's second marriage had also been troubled, and Christine served him with divorce papers on the last day of January 1982. There were allegations that Randy had hit her. As an adult she was free to remove herself from a bad situation, but Christine worried about leaving the two-year-old behind. She took her concerns to her lawyer, David Krizensky, who in turn contacted the Neenah police. "In the past Randy has hit the boy causing marks and is a prime case for child abuse," the complaint reads. "Christine is afraid that when she leaves next Monday and leaves the boy alone with Randy something may happen." Krizensky then contacted DSS, where a file on the family was begun by a caseworker named Peter Donner. The agency investigated the situation but, according to the case notes, concluded that "Randy had given physical custody of Joshua to Joshua's grandfather living in Stevens Point so services were not needed." The social worker did not investigate the circumstances that had led Randy to hand the boy over to his father's care, nor did he arrange to have a DSS worker in Portage County visit the home to check on Joshua. For reasons that are not clear from the public record, the boy soon returned to live with Randy in Neenah. For awhile Joshua and his father lived out of Randy's van. During that time Randy met Marie DeShaney, the former wife of his half-brother, Mark DeShaney, and the two set up a household in an apartment in Neenah that consisted of Randy, Marie, Joshua, and Marie's son, Rusty, who was six months old. On January 22, 1983, almost exactly one year after Christine had warned DSS about her concerns for Joshua, the child made his first trip to the emergency room at Theda Clark Regional Medical Center in Neenah.

Joshua was brought to the hospital at 1:30 that January afternoon by Marie, who identified herself to hospital personnel as the little boy's aunt. A friend had driven them to the emergency room because another toddler, a boy named Andy, had struck Joshua with a metal toy truck. He had a three-inch abrasion on his forehead that had swollen markedly, protruding a half-inch. The emergency room staff became suspicious about Marie's explanation of how the accident had happened. Their doubts were furthered when Marie objected to a nurse removing Joshua's clothing. A nurse took Joshua to be x-rayed, and when his clothes were removed, she saw numerous additional injuries on the child's body, apparently of differing ages. In addition to a quarter-sized bruise on his face, the boy had several injuries to his scalp and spine, and numerous bruises on both buttocks and upper thighs as well as the penis, ankle, and heel. Perhaps most disturbing were the marks on both of the buttocks and the right arm, with a distinctive pattern of indentations; the nurse thought the marks may have been made by the bristles of a hairbrush. According to a report filed by Robert E. Gehringer, a pediatrician who saw Joshua in the emergency room, when Joshua had been asked about his injuries, he said "my daddy spanks us with the belt." The nurse telephoned Theda Clark's medical social worker, Thomas Hoare, as per the hospital's protocol when a case of child abuse was suspected.

Hoare arrived at the emergency room and noted for himself the multiple bruises and the unusual patterned marks on the child's buttocks and arm. After consulting with Gehringer, and questioning Marie himself, Hoare decided to contact the Winnebago County DSS office in Oshkosh about the suspected abuse. It was a Saturday, and Donner, the caseworker who had started the DeShaney family file after Christine's complaint, was unavailable. But another child protective worker from a DSS branch office in Neenah, Ann Kemmeter, lived in town, and Hoare was able to reach her at home. Kemmeter, who had been employed with the Winnebago County DSS since 1967, came to the hospital and also became suspicious about the nature of the child's injuries. Further, she thought the bristle-like marks may have been inflicted by Marie, a woman who once described herself as "big and strong." Randy was out of town on an ice fishing trip and the DSS worker felt leery about allowing Joshua to leave the hospital with Marie. Invoking the authority the State of Wisconsin invested in her, Kemmeter contacted the intake worker of the juvenile court about having the state take emergency custody of Joshua. The petition was granted and Joshua was admitted into the hospital's pediatric unit just after 4:00 P.M. Hoare asked the pediatrics staff to observe interactions between Joshua and his father when he came to visit his son.

Randy arrived that evening, reportedly very upset. Detective Keith Nelson of the Neenah Police Department came to the hospital and, along with the DSS child protective worker, conducted interviews with both Randy and Marie after advising them of their Miranda rights. Both denied abusing Joshua, and they told Nelson that they had been intending to contact Gehringer in any case because he seemed to bruise easily and the injuries failed to heal quickly. Randy was especially concerned about this because his sister had died of leukemia when Randy was sixteen. Kemmeter seemed reassured by their explanations, recording in her notes that "Detective Nelson and myself found Marie DeShaney and Randy DeShaney to be very cooperative in the sharing of information." The two were interviewed again on Monday by Kemmeter, this time accompanied by Hoare. "Once again they were very cooperative and very open to sharing information with us," Kemmeter later wrote in a report to the juvenile court, "and there appeared to be no basis to the establishment of child abuse or neglect. Rather," she continued, "it appeared they were lacking in parenting skills and may not have provided adequate supervision to Joshua and two other children Marie takes care of." (Marie was a caregiver to Joshua, Rusty, and Andy, her friend's son.) The child protective worker then learned that Joshua's behavior appeared to be deteriorating of late. Although he had been potty trained when he lived with Randy and Christine, the three-year-old had begun wetting his bed (a condition called "enuresis") and soiling himself (known as "encopresis," a condition often associated with psychological disturbances). Randy and Marie told her that he was also playing more roughly, biting and pinching himself and pulling out his own hair, leaving bloody marks on his scalp. A few days earlier he had twisted his own ear so severely it had turned purple. When Marie had asked Joshua why he did it, the boy told her he pulled his own ear because the baby, Rusty, also did it to himself. They thought the bruise on Joshua's penis may have resulted from the child pinching himself as well. They added that Joshua became especially agitated when Randy left the apartment, and during the previous week Randy had gone ice fishing on three separate days, so Joshua had been quite unmanageable. In light of this information, Gehringer called in Donald Derozier, a psychologist, to examine Joshua. Derozier interviewed Randy as well.

Wisconsin's child protection laws, originally enacted in 1955 and subsequently modified in 1977, were known as Chapter 48, or the Children's Code. Under the statutes, the ultimate responsibility for determining whether a child could be removed permanently from his parents' home fell to the juvenile court. Court action was initiated by a petition filed by the county social service agency. Kemmeter, in her role as a Winnebago County child protective worker, and John Bodnar, the county's assistant corporation counsel, were the individuals responsible for making the request based on evidence from an investigation of the child's home and family circumstances, as required by the Children's Code. On Tuesday, Hoare convened a "child protective team meeting" at the hospital to share and discuss the evidence that had been gathered about the DeShaney family's situation. A number of professionals participated, including Bodnar, Nelson, Gehringer, Derozier, emergency room staff, nurses from the pediatric unit, and Kemmeter, along with her DSS supervisor, Cheryl Stelse.

Nurses in the hospital's pediatrics unit reported observing a good relationship between Joshua and Randy. Joshua did not seem at all afraid of his father, they had noticed; in fact, he ran to him with his arms out wanting to jump up and be hugged when Randy arrived at the unit. The psychologist, Derozier, reported that he had administered the Stanford-Binet intelligence scale tests and had measured Joshua's IQ at 113, a score in the "bright normal" range. He described the boy as "bright and alert," with an appropriate attention span for his age. However, when Joshua was shown "projective pictures" and asked to describe them, Derozier reported that he "invariably ended up with negative conclusions. Children either die, houses burn down, etc." This evidence, in addition to the information that Joshua became extremely agitated when Randy left the house, led Derozier to hypothesize that the child "does have significant anxiety with reference to the instability of the home situation." He had found Randy to be "fairly attentive to the child." He had learned from his interview that Randy's own father was an alcoholic and Randy himself "may have been [an alcoholic] in the past." Joshua's father had also told the psychologist that he suspected Melody had abused the child when he was still in her custody. According to Kemmeter's meeting notes, Derozier told the team that neglect and abuse in his infancy could account for the three-year-old's apparent self-destructive behavior. The psychologist recommended that both Randy and Joshua should "be seen professionally" to address the boy's problems. He suggested that Joshua be enrolled in a program like Head Start to help further his psychological and cognitive development. Participation in Head Start would also make the child visible to adults outside of the DeShaney household. Gehringer added that he would like to follow Joshua's situation via his position as a pediatrician at the Nicolet Clinic in Neenah.

Detective Nelson, however, had reservations about allowing Joshua to return to his father's home. Nelson was skeptical of the various explanations Randy and Marie had given for Joshua's injuries. He had tried to talk to Joshua in the hospital but had not succeeded in getting "anything definite out of him; [Joshua] would tend to agree with anything you say, both negative or positive," he wrote in his notes. Nelson thought the patterned marks on Joshua's body resembled the surface of a ping-pong paddle, but when he had investigated the home none had been found. The police officer's notes paint a disturbing picture of the DeShaney household. Randy admitted to Nelson that both he and Marie spanked Joshua "when he needs it" with their hands, and he himself used a belt on occasion, but Randy stressed that he never used the buckle end. They cited as an example of Joshua "needing" to be spanked an incident that had occurred a few days before his hospital admission. On that day, they told the detective, Joshua had wet his pants twice and therefore Randy had disciplined him with a spanking. Marie said that Joshua lately had been playing Superman and jumping from his bed into his toy box, and speculated that this boisterous play may have caused some of his injuries. Marie also told Nelson that a few days previously Joshua had fallen on the sidewalk twice while they were walking to the grocery store, which may have explained the extensive bruising on his legs.

The detective then asked her when Joshua had last been bathed. Marie replied that she had given Joshua a bath the night before his emergency room visit, but asserted she had not noticed any unusual bruising at that time. Nor did Joshua appear to have such marks when he had come out of his bedroom that morning, including the quarter-sized bruise on his face. Nelson asked to see the toy truck with which

Joshua reportedly had been struck in the head. Upon examining the toy, Nelson concluded that "it would seem that this toy, being swung hard by a two-year-old, couldn't produce such a large swelled bump as I witnessed yesterday, but I couldn't say without some doubt that it is virtually impossible." To him, the wound looked as if the child's head had come into contact with a hard surface, such as a wall or a floor. Nelson also spoke with the DeShaneys' neighbors in the apartment building. One neighbor told him that she often heard a little child crying "almost all day long" but could not identify which of the two little boys it was, nor was she certain if the crying was the result of the child being struck by one of the adults in the apartment. Another neighbor reported hearing Randy "swearing and yelling" but could not confirm hearing anything indicating a beating was taking place.

Although the detective lacked confidence in the various explanations given for Joshua's injuries, he had not uncovered solid evidence that the child was being physically abused, and whether the abuser was Randy, Marie, or both, and therefore no arrest could be made at the time. But Nelson remained concerned for Joshua's safety. "My own kids have had bruises on their arms," he recalled in a deposition several years later, "and they have fallen on their knees, but I couldn't believe that this number of injuries should be normal, whether it was abuse of the child himself or some destructive qualities or problems, and I just felt that definitely he should . . . have protection for his safety against whatever is causing this [and] should be removed or monitored." Despite his concerns, however, under Wisconsin law Nelson did not have the authority to remove Joshua from the DeShaney home. According to Nelson, although "a police officer's opinion can sway what a social worker may do or not do . . . [child protective workers] have to make the final decision as to whether they want to sign that form. A police officer cannot take custody that I know of without their okay." At the team meeting, Nelson voiced his opinion that "the situation is in need of close supervision by the Department of Social Services and I would hope an ongoing physical surveillance by the hospital and Social Services be started for Joshua." Nelson's observations, as it happened, were prescient.

Ultimately, as Kemmeter reported in her memo to the juvenile court, corporation counsel Bodnar advised the child protective team that there was not sufficient evidence of abuse to petition the juvenile

{ *Chapter 1* }

court to keep Joshua in the state's custody. The boy was released from the hospital in the care of Randy later that day. Bodnar's cautious approach may have been the result of a lawsuit filed in Wisconsin just three years earlier, *Roe v. Borup*, in which the parents of a child removed from their home because of social workers' suspicions of sexual abuse sued the Dodge County Department of Social Services after it was discovered that the allegations had been unfounded. But there were conditions to Joshua's release. Randy entered into a voluntary "social service" agreement with DSS; such a voluntary agreement, although written and signed by both parties, was distinct from a mandate ordered by the court, in which the provisions would have the force of law. The terms of the DSS agreement were as follows: Joshua would be enrolled in Head Start and Randy would "work with the department to increase his knowledge of child development as well as to increase his parenting skills." The DSS also informed Randy that they believed it best that Marie move out of the house. Kemmeter noted that Randy indicated he was "accepting of any and all help that would be made available to him." The child protective worker was optimistic that she could work cooperatively with the DeShaneys to resolve the family's problems. DSS would provide services on a "voluntary" basis and, although Wisconsin law gave her the authority to determine whether it was safe for Joshua to remain in Randy's home, Kemmeter envisioned her role in the DeShaney case from this point on as being more therapeutic than authoritative. She was keenly aware of the fact that, just as Randy had entered into the social service agreement voluntarily, he could also choose to withdraw, severing contacts between Joshua and DSS. If Randy did not want her in his home, she later told a local newspaper, "he could have demanded that she leave." She believed it was in the child's best interest to keep the door to the DeShaney home open to her supervision and planned to make monthly visits to check on the family's progress. On February 14, 1983, the Winnebago County juvenile court closed the child protective case on Joshua.

Although in the harsh light of history Kemmeter's optimism about Joshua's future seems sadly misplaced, she was not inexperienced in the field of child protection. Kemmeter was working in her hometown, a small town in Wisconsin's Fox River Valley, the place where she had grown up and felt comfortable. A 1961 graduate of Neenah

High School, she had completed a bachelor of arts degree in psychology at the University of Wisconsin–Oshkosh in 1966 and worked for a time in Bethesda, Maryland. But she missed her home in the Midwest and soon returned to Wisconsin, where she worked for the Winnebago County Department of Social Services while she continued her professional training at the University of Wisconsin–Madison, receiving a bachelor of arts in social work in 1971 and a master of science in social work the following year. Two years later, in 1974, Kemmeter became the supervisor of the Child Protective Services Unit for Winnebago County. She had served in that capacity for ten years when she took on the responsibility of healing the DeShaneys. Another DSS supervisor would later tell a local newspaper that Kemmeter was "one of our very best employees." Perhaps Kemmeter's experience in child protection work, and her intimate familiarity with the Neenah community, led her to feel confident that the voluntary social service agreement Randy entered into with DSS would be an effective means for securing Joshua's safety.

On a follow-up visit to the DeShaney home ten days after Joshua's release from the hospital, Kemmeter noted in her files that Randy was not present in the home, but Marie was. This must have been disconcerting to the social worker, since it had been her own suspicions that Marie may have been harming Joshua that had led her to initiate proceedings for the state taking temporary custody of the child. In addition the psychologist, Derozier, had determined that Marie's continued presence was detrimental to Joshua, and DSS had expressed as much to Randy when they released Joshua to his custody. Marie told Kemmeter that Randy and Joshua would be spending two weeks visiting Randy's father in Stevens Point, and Kemmeter arranged to visit again upon their return. That date's entry in her official report ends with the following notations:

Goal — PROTECTION
Primary Objective — RESOLUTION OF ABUSE, NEGLECT, OR EXPLOITATION
Service Area — INDIVIDUAL AND FAMILY ADJUSTMENT
Role — COUNSELING
I will continue to provide counseling services to Randy to improve his knowledge of child development and parenting skills.

Service Area — EDUCATION

Role — ADVOCATE

I will advocate either a pre-school or Headstart [sic] Program, in which Joshua could participate to improve his intellectual and social skills.

Service Area — EMPLOYMENT RELATED

I will advocate for full-time employment for Randy in having him explore possible job opportunities. He is presently exploring the possibility of employment in Florida, although nothing has materialized to date.

Service Area — HEALTH RELATED

I will advocate sound health care practices for Joshua and monitor to be sure that he gets in for his bi-monthly exams with Dr. Gehringer.

Note here that Kemmeter's stated goal was *protection* and her stated objective *resolution of abuse, neglect, or exploitation*. Yet she identified her own role as that of *counselor* and *advocate* — not as that of an authority or law enforcement figure. Her job title within DSS remained "child protective worker," but under the voluntary agreement between DSS and Randy she would take on a helping, rather than an authoritative, role. She planned to work with Randy to "improve his knowledge of child development and parenting skills," although what this work would consist of was not explicated in her notes. Marie later told police that Kemmeter "gives advice to her on how to take care of the kids." The social worker also planned to assist Randy in finding him a full-time job. Joshua would go to Head Start to "improve his intellectual and social skills," and Kemmeter herself — again in the role of "advocate" — would ensure that the child received regular pediatric checkups.

Kemmeter's notes provide a clear illustration of the "family preservation" model that had become a core tenet of professional social work by the 1980s (see Chapter Two). The model was based on an underlying assumption that the private family, rather than the state, was under most circumstances the desirable caretaker of children. The model had also arisen from widespread dissatisfaction with state foster care systems. Under the family preservation paradigm, domestic violence resulted from families' lack of sufficient resources for providing the proper environment in which individual members could function adequately. Thus the state's responsibility for protecting children extended beyond policing violent adult behavior. Social workers were to serve as intermediaries between the private household and the state's social welfare bureaucracy. Under this model, a successful outcome for Joshua would be his continued residence in his father's home, but a home made more secure and conducive to normal child development with an infusion of state social services such as parenting classes, child development programs, and job counseling. As the family's caseworker, Kemmeter's role was to inform, advise, and counsel Randy, enabling him to better fulfill his responsibilities to his son. This required her to maintain an open and at least cordial relationship with the DeShaney household, remaining sensitive to the family's interpersonal dynamics and aware of any changes in its economic and social situation. If the State of Wisconsin provided a "safety net" of social services to troubled families like the DeShaneys, Kemmeter herself was the designated "life line" connecting the state to the private household.

But the web of interconnections between public and private realms was further complicated by the social worker's parallel role as the state's eyes and ears in determining whether Joshua remained safe in his father's home. Under the Wisconsin Children's Code, she was authorized — indeed required — to investigate, interrogate, and keep household members under the state's surveillance. This law enforcement role necessitated a different sort of relationship between the state and the DeShaneys, one in which the DSS worker would assume authority and initiate action to protect the child should the situation call for it. Kemmeter herself acknowledged as much in the memorandum she had written to the juvenile court while Joshua was in the hospital. Although recommending that the temporary custody the state had assumed be dismissed, Kemmeter had added that she "will refer it back into Court should there be any further injuries to this child of an unexplained origin." Thus the social worker's position was a profoundly ambiguous one. Although her function as counselor and advocate on the family's behalf required her to gain their trust and cooperation, her simultaneous responsibility as Joshua's protector demanded that she abruptly change direction and assume the role of enforcer of state law if so required. Whether Kemmeter could have known when it was time to make such a shift in roles became a central dispute in the civil lawsuit that eventually came before the U.S. Supreme Court. In any case, the social worker did not relinquish her therapeutic role, with tragic results.

On July 25, 1983, seven months after Joshua's release from the hospital, Kemmeter placed a social service review in the DeShaney file. The report noted that she had made a total of four visits to the home; three additional appointments had been canceled by the family. In June the DeShaneys, including Marie and her son Rusty, had moved to Oshkosh, Wisconsin, 15 miles south of Neenah, where they rented a small two-bedroom bungalow-style house in an older section of the city. Randy said he wanted to move away from Neenah because both his mother and his ex-wife Christine lived there, and he did not get along with either woman. Interestingly, Kemmeter continued her social service arrangement with Randy rather than handing over the case to a DSS worker in Oshkosh, even though it would now require her to drive 30 miles round-trip for the monthly home visits. It also placed the child protective worker further away from the close supervision of the child she had undertaken to shield from danger. And, although the voluntary agreement had been with Randy alone, Marie was still very much in the picture. "Randy had, at one time, felt it would be in Joshua's best interest if he and Marie no longer lived together," Kemmeter noted in her six-month review. "Randy, apparently, has changed his mind as he and Marie, along with her son, Rusty, and Joshua continue to reside as a family unit. Both Randy and Marie feel that there is some improvement in their relationships since they have moved away from the Tupper family in Neenah." (The Tuppers were a couple consisting of the brother of Christine DeShaney and his wife. Christine was Randy's ex-wife.) "Both also feel that it was Andy, Joshua's playmate, who caused much of Joshua's beatings and lacerations." Kemmeter recorded these items as facts, without evaluation or analysis on her part. Both DeShaneys had presented an upbeat prognosis to the social worker. Relocating to a new town, away from the negative influences of others outside of their household, the DeShaneys could now function more happily as a family. The problem, they implied, had been their former environment in Neenah, not their own actions or behavior.

But Kemmeter also noted her concern that Joshua continued to have "accidents." Two months after his release from Theda Clark

Regional Medical Center in January, she received a call from Hoare notifying her that the boy had returned to the emergency room where he received stitches to another laceration on his forehead. Marie later told police that the cut was the result of Joshua crawling under his bed and hitting his head on the metal bed frame. On a home visit several weeks later Kemmeter noted a bump on Joshua's forehead that was explained (the notes aren't clear by whom) as the result of a fall off a tricycle. Although she concluded that "there is enough of the accident-prone syndrome present for me to continue to want to follow this family for awhile," Kemmeter was not particularly alarmed.

Despite these concerns, Kemmeter's report makes it clear that she was hopeful about the family's future that summer. Randy continued to look for full-time employment and the social worker observed that he "seems to be more attentive to Joshua, with a noted behavioral improvement." Randy was an avid fisherman, and he had begun taking his son with him on fishing trips. Although Joshua had not yet been enrolled in Head Start, Kemmeter was satisfied with Randy's assurance that he planned to contact the program in Oshkosh. "Basically, the DeShaneys continue to remain cooperative and appear to be honest in discussing Joshua's behavior and his accidents," she wrote. "I will continue to monitor this family for another six months, to monitor the accidents, as well as to suggest service areas which may be in their best interest." Thus Kemmeter strove to maintain what she perceived as an open relationship with the DeShaneys, persisting in her role as their counselor and advocate, continuing to serve as the vital link between this struggling family and the state's social service bureaucracy in Winnebago County. The couple's apparent cooperation and honesty in their relationship were, for Kemmeter, indications of her progress in working with them.

Yet there is something distinctly unsettling about the social worker's report. It is worth observing that she used the term "accidents" repeatedly in the notes. She did not reveal any concerns she may have had that Joshua's self-induced injuries were in themselves possible indications of physical abuse, a syndrome well established by child abuse experts at the time. Instead, the social worker remained focused on the adult DeShaneys' need to learn better parenting skills to lessen Joshua's tendency to harm himself. Kemmeter believed that Randy and Marie had inappropriate behavioral expectations for Joshua who, now four years of age, made his own bed in the mornings, folded his pajamas, bathed and dressed himself, and when hungry prepared peanut butter and jelly sandwiches without adult assistance. Significantly, since the 1970s experts in the field of child welfare had identified outsized expectations for children's behavior as a common personality trait among adults who abuse children. A 1972 volume, *Helping the Battered Child and His Family*, for example, explained that abusive parents share a common pattern of child rearing "characterized by a high demand for the child to perform so as to gratify the parents, and by the use of severe physical punishment to ensure the child's proper behavior." Such adults may also attribute inappropriately sophisticated and devious motives to children's misbehavior. In addition, several members of the child protection team — including Kemmeter herself — had expressed grave concerns about the possibility that Marie was abusing Joshua, but she remained in the household caring for the boy. Marie apparently spent a considerable amount of time alone with the little boys. The couple revealed that Randy had left them for several weeks to drive a truck with his father, and had spent some time in Florida as well. It is striking that, although Kemmeter's report is confident in tone, in fact Randy had not followed through with even one of the recommendations in the social service agreement made seven months earlier. He was still out of work, Joshua had not been enrolled in Head Start, and injuries continued to appear on the child's body with disconcerting frequency. Whether the child protective worker could have realized it based on the facts she had at hand, in reality the DeShaney home was a dangerous place for the little boy, and indeed the violence appeared to be escalating.

The DeShaneys moved to Oshkosh in June 1983, and over the following months police responded to domestic violence complaints at their home six times. The police contacted DSS on September 14 because a neighbor had witnessed Marie slapping Joshua repeatedly, reportedly so hard that the child was falling to the ground. (Marie later told police that she was disciplining Joshua because he kept trying to run away from her into the street.) Later that month, Joshua made another trip to the emergency room, this time at Mercy hospital in Oshkosh, for a corneal abrasion. At that time Marie told the attendants that Joshua had unexpectedly grabbed a bottle of liquid detergent and squeezed some soap into his eye before she could take it from him. In October, Kemmeter noted in the case file another injury she observed during a home visit, a swelling she described as a "large goose bump" on Joshua's left forehead. At the following month's visit, on November 9, she observed what she thought were cigarette burns on the boy's neck and chin, and she asked Marie about the marks. When Marie told Joshua to explain to the social worker how he had come to be injured, the child replied that he had knelt down on his hands and knees and rubbed his own face on the sidewalk. Again, there is no indication in the case notes that Kemmeter thought this disturbing incident — whether the boy's wounds were cigarette burns or self-induced abrasions — required immediate further investigation.

Nor was the violence in the DeShaney home restricted to Joshua's injuries. The Oshkosh police went to the home twice on November 11 and then again the following day to investigate what was apparently a sustained physical fight between Randy and Marie, leaving Marie with a very badly bruised eye. (Several weeks later, Randy again beat Marie; this time her injury required her to receive stitches in her lip.) Throughout this period of turmoil in the DeShaney household, neither Kemmeter nor any other social service employees reported any suspicions that Rusty was also being abused, although later the Oshkosh police would record witness testimony that Randy had in fact done so; it should be noted, however, that Randy was never legally charged with abusing Rusty. On November 30 Joshua appeared again at the emergency room at Mercy hospital, this time for yet another laceration on his forehead, and the attendees who examined him also noted blood in his left nostril, a red and swollen left ear, and injuries to both shoulders. When they confronted Randy, he explained that Joshua fell in the bathroom and hit his head on the toilet. Subsequently, however, Randy gave a different explanation. A friend who visited the DeShaneys one week later told Oshkosh police she had observed the stitches in Joshua's forehead and had asked Randy what had happened to the child. According to this witness, Randy replied that Joshua had soiled his pants and Marie had ordered him to clean up. Randy and Marie had begun punishing Joshua by requiring him to wash his own pants in the sink when he soiled them. This time the child refused and Marie struck him, knocking him into the bathroom sink. The friend said that Marie then said she "hated" Joshua and "she was afraid she would hurt him or maybe even kill him in the future." Although, of course, the reader should not assume that such witness testimony is factually accurate, this statement is only one of many similar accounts that the Oshkosh police gathered about the violence that was occurring in the DeShaney household during the period from July 1983 to March 1984. One officer, Paul Michler, later said that upon being called to the home by neighbors during one dispute he had spoken with Joshua himself and at the time the officer had become concerned for the child's safety. It should be noted, however, that whether Michler's report ever reached Kemmeter remained a disputed fact in the civil suit.

Emergency room staff at Mercy hospital did, however, make note of their suspicions when they treated Joshua on November 30. The physician who examined Joshua and stitched his head wound was Timothy Bowers. Wisconsin law required that a report regarding any suspicious injury to a child treated in a hospital be submitted to a social service agency. At Mercy hospital, the procedure consisted of completing a form and sending it to the hospital's social services department. Bowers, however, did not complete the form himself; instead, he asked an attending nurse to undertake the task. Following protocol, she sent the report to the hospital social worker, Ann Marshall, who in turn contacted DSS. Kemmeter noted the incident in a social service review dated almost two months later, on January 25, 1984, although it is unclear from the record at what point she had actually learned that the injury to Joshua had taken place. At a future deposition, the emergency room physician would explain that, under the circumstances, he would not have made a "diagnosis" of child abuse in any case; unlike a patient presenting with chest pain, there were no objective medical tests to determine the cause of Joshua's symptoms. Bowers recalled he did not believe the four-year-old boy was in immediate danger at the time, despite the rather unusual extent of his injuries, and had seen no problem in releasing him to Randy and Marie.

But, according to his deposition, the doctor had other reasons for avoiding reporting the incident as well. As an emergency room physician he felt he didn't have time to fill out forms. (In a subsequent deposition, Ann Marshall said that the Mercy hospital medical staff submitted approximately two or three such forms every month.)

Three nurses were in attendance in the emergency room that day, and because he was required to see every patient himself, he needed "to keep moving." Interestingly, he also acknowledged that he had been hesitant to put his signature on the form because he knew it meant he might be called to give testimony at a later date, perhaps at a child protective team meeting in the hospital, something he did not think he had time for given his intense schedule at the emergency room. "The nurse has a lot of people covering for her," Bowers averred. "If she's called to testify, she'll be reimbursed by the hospital. That's paid. She has someone else to cover for her and it's absolutely no problem for them [sic] to get the time." Bowers did not believe that delegating the reporting to a nurse had been in any way inappropriate. "No one came back to me and said, 'you should have done this,'" he explained. He had felt under no legal or professional obligation to follow up on the case after treating and releasing Joshua.

On January 9, 1984, Ruth Davis, the local Head Start director in Oshkosh, arrived at the DeShaney's house to inquire about Joshua. Davis was aware of the social service agreement Randy had made with DSS a full year earlier, but the boy had never been enrolled in the program as per its terms. To her dismay, Davis found the four-year-old home alone. She attempted to contact Kemmeter, leaving a message with the DSS receptionist that afternoon, although Kemmeter did not receive it until the following day. Davis did not try to contact another DSS child protective worker, nor did she file a report with the Oshkosh police. Recalling that day in a subsequent deposition, Marie said that the family wanted to make a call to Randy's father, but because they had no telephone service in their home, they had to walk to a pay phone three blocks away. According to her testimony, Joshua said he "just wanted to take a nap and sleep." The adults were not concerned about leaving him alone because they didn't think he would get into trouble. (They did take Rusty along.) She explained that the trip had only taken fifteen minutes. Davis, Marie surmised, had arrived at the house coincidentally within that short window of time. Later, however, when Davis did manage to make contact with the DeShaneys, they refused to enroll Joshua in Head Start. Kemmeter's notes indicate that Davis reported the incident to DSS and that Randy and Marie were aware they had been reported for leaving Joshua alone; thus, it is likely that they mistrusted Davis and refused further cooperation with her. Although Kemmeter was undoubtedly disappointed, Randy's agreement to enroll Joshua in Head Start had been "voluntary" and thus could not be enforced. The child protective worker observed in her case notes, again rather optimistically given the boy's circumstances, that Joshua would be turning five in March and therefore would be eligible to begin kindergarten in the fall.

Kemmeter's social service review for January 1984 reflected for the first time her growing doubts about the true nature of Joshua's "accidents." A year after her first encounter with the DeShaneys at Theda Clark Regional Medical Center in Neenah, the numerous injuries to Joshua (three involving trips to the emergency room), and several police reports of domestic violence in the home, the social worker was now willing to consider the possibility that the boy's frequent injuries were not caused solely by rough play or self-destructive actions, but instead by one or possibly two abusive adults. She asked another worker at DSS, Christine Howe Feakes, to join her on the case. But despite her uncertainty, Kemmeter still hesitated to assume the role of law enforcer. "I am not certain who the abuser of Joshua would be," she speculated in her case notes. "However, I cannot help but hypothesize that the probability of Randy becoming upset with Marie — using physical violence, and Marie not knowing what to do with her frustrations, and anger, possibly taking them out on Joshua." Kemmeter attached to her review the police reports on the domestic violence incidents between Randy and Marie that had taken place the previous November. Nevertheless, her notes indicate that she found it difficult to relinquish the role of therapist, speculating about the family's emotional dynamics and analyzing the ways in which the state could address its needs. "We will make continued attempts to improve the parenting skills within this family unit," she wrote, "and to lower their expectations of Joshua's behavior and general motor development skills." Although she was becoming suspicious about the true nature of Joshua's injuries, Kemmeter had not altered her original view that the real threat to the boy's safety was Marie, not his father. She believed she had developed a good working relationship with Randy, and was confident that she had built a solid foundation of trust with the family. Ruth Davis of Head Start had already "frightened the family away" by reporting them to DSS. A close reading of her case notes suggests that Kemmeter may have had difficulty reconciling the

Randy DeShaney she knew as an agreeable and cooperative client, interested in improving his parenting skills and finding help for Joshua's behavioral problems, with the mounting indications that he may in fact have been a perpetrator of domestic violence.

When Kemmeter arrived for her scheduled home visit later that January, she was informed that Joshua was in bed with the flu and the adults did not want him disturbed. She did not insist on seeing him (something Wisconsin law empowered child protective workers to do) nor did she reschedule her visit for later that month. Arriving in February, Kemmeter found no one at home. If the social worker believed the DeShaneys were deliberately avoiding contact with her (as they had already rejected Ruth Davis of Head Start), she did not indicate as much in her notes. Marie would later tell the Oshkosh police that she had begun resenting Kemmeter because Joshua's behavior became worse after the social worker's visits. When Kemmeter left the house, according to Marie, Joshua "wanted to go with her." A few weeks later, on March 3, Marie was treated at the Mercy hospital emergency room for a split lip and a broken nose, the result of another fight with Randy.

Kemmeter made another attempt to visit the DeShaney home on March 7, 1984. Although she had noted her concerns that Joshua was a possible victim of child abuse in her January review, she had not actually seen the boy since November 9, a full four months earlier. Kemmeter appears to have changed her strategy for dealing with the DeShaneys because, unlike her previous calls, this time Kemmeter arrived at their home unannounced. Later, she dictated into her notes her own recollection of what had taken place during that March visit:

> It was Rusty's second birthday and Marie and Randy were in the kitchen decorating his birthday cake. I wrote Happy Birthday Rusty on the cake and Randy finished decorating. Both Marie and Randy seemed to be at ease and told me there were fewer fights and they were getting along much better. . . . [Marie told Kemmeter that her stitches were due to "nose surgery for some type of blockage." If the social worker was suspicious of the explanation, she did not indicate so in her notes.] Rusty and Joshua were taking a nap. Joshua had woken up. Marie went back to his bedroom quieting him down and then came back to the kitchen where we all were. I don't know why but I did not ask to see Joshua. All appeared to be okay and a relaxed

atmosphere in the household. They did mention that Joshua had fainted several days earlier in the bathroom for no apparent reason.

Despite the disturbing revelation about Joshua's fainting, and Marie's facial injuries, Kemmeter's report describes a tranquil scene in the DeShaney household. She joined in the domestic ritual of decorating Rusty's cake. She noted that Randy was cleaning fish for dinner, and even added the detail that he was carefully removing the bones so the children would not choke on them. The DeShaneys said they were expecting friends later that evening who were coming to help celebrate Rusty's birthday. By her account, Kemmeter stayed about forty-five minutes and then drove the 15 miles back to Neenah. Apparently still regarding her relationship with the DeShaneys as a voluntary social service agreement, and perhaps because she believed that Randy and Marie had been open and honest in their previous encounters, Kemmeter did not invoke her legal authority as a child protective worker and insist upon seeing Joshua that evening, although she had been told he had fainted. She did not advise them to seek medical treatment for the child. Marie claimed that she had told Kemmeter that Joshua had been throwing up the previous day, but the social worker had "ignored her." (It should be noted that Marie made this statement to police when she herself was under investigation for abusing Joshua.)

The following evening, March 8, Kemmeter received a telephone call from a nurse at Mercy hospital. The nurse informed her that Joshua had been brought to the emergency room, this time with a severe head injury. Kemmeter asked if a DSS worker in Oshkosh could take the call, but was told that she had been requested specifically, although it is not clear from the record who had made the request. The social worker drove the 15 miles from Neenah that evening. Arriving at Mercy, she was met by the nurse, the hospital's chaplain, Marie, and her son, Rusty. They told her that Randy was with Joshua, who was undergoing a CAT scan. (A CAT, or computerized axial tomography, scan is an x-ray procedure that, with the aid of a computer, provides three-dimensional views of the body.) Kemmeter asked Marie what had happened to the boy, and Marie told her that Joshua had fallen down the basement stairs in their home. He had been brought into the emergency room unconscious by Randy and Marie. Kemmeter spoke separately with the nurse and hospital chaplain, who revealed that Randy had been quite violent when the DeShaneys arrived, "pounding on the doors and walls." They worried that he would strike one of the hospital staff. Randy then returned from Joshua's CAT scan; he was, in Kemmeter's words, "crying, shaking, and speaking very loudly," a reaction she attributed to stress and grief. The social worker took Randy to a small lounge area and, at her request, he was given an injection of the sedative Haldol by a nurse. Then she called the Oshkosh police.

At that point Kemmeter went to see Joshua, whom she found in an appalling condition. An array of tubes covered his face, and the child was breathing through a hand respirator being operated by a nurse. Both eyes had been taped shut. Through the tubes and tape Kemmeter could make out severe bruising on both of Joshua's cheeks and along the base of his throat. The nurse told her that the CAT scan had revealed hemorrhaging in the boy's brain, and he was being prepared for emergency neurosurgery to relieve pressure from the swelling. Returning to Randy and Marie, she asked Randy to accompany her to meet with the police detectives. "He cooperated," Kemmeter later wrote, "but expressed concern as to why it was necessary as Joshua's injuries were an accident and again told me he had fallen down the stairs and again said to me, 'Ann, you know Joshua bruises easily.'" But this time the magnitude of physical harm far surpassed the child's previous injuries. Tests had revealed blood in Joshua's urine, and physicians were trying to determine whether there were broken bones or internal injuries in addition to the apparently severe head injury. They told Kemmeter that Joshua's chances of surviving the neurosurgery that night were only about 25 percent. Kemmeter called Cheryl Stelse, her DSS supervisor, to let her know about Joshua's condition; she also asked Stelse to bring the DeShaney case file so that the Oshkosh detectives could begin an investigation.

Kemmeter's description of events, written in her social service review four months later, demonstrate her continued concern for the well-being of Randy. (By the time she submitted the report, Randy had been arrested for Joshua's beating.) She described her attempts to calm him down from the highly distressed state in which she had found him upon arriving at Mercy hospital. "He was crying, and shaking, and speaking very loudly," she wrote. "He told me Joshua is his whole life and that if anything happened to Josh he would have no reason to live and mentioned the possibility of suicide." She also observed that Marie's behavior differed considerably from Randy's. "It should also be noted during the entire time I was at the hospital that night that Marie remained controlled," the social worker wrote. "While she was shaking from time to time and appeared tense, at no time did I see her cry or express sadness/remorse over the situation." Apparently, Marie remained the object of Kemmeter's suspicions. She also made it a point to look carefully at Rusty, but recorded in her notes that she saw no signs of physical abuse on the boy.

Marc Letellier, a neurosurgeon, spoke to the group after the surgery. He revealed that the extent of swelling in Joshua's brain (the CAT scan showed the hemorrhage nearly covered the entire right hemisphere) had required the removal of a large section of the skull. The child had been moved to the intensive care unit, and Letellier informed them that "it could be weeks before Joshua would wake up if he did at all." Randy, Marie, and Rusty then returned home. Kemmeter stayed, however, and an impromptu meeting was held with Letellier, his nurse, emergency room personnel, Stelse, and the Oshkosh police detectives. Letellier told them that, although the bleeding in Joshua's brain had been severe, he had been able to stop it and remove the pooled blood. After suctioning he had found a clot so large that it had actually depressed the brain downward in the skull. The surgeon had also noticed a number of older bruises on Joshua's shaved head. Upon removing the section of the skull, he saw several deposits of bilirubin within the boy's brain, a substance left behind when blood had been reabsorbed into the brain tissue. This, along with the bruises on the scalp, indicated to the neurosurgeon that numerous such seepages had occurred on previous occasions. Significantly, Letellier did not find any external points of impact — the kinds of cuts or abrasions that one would expect to find had the child fallen down the stairs, as the DeShaneys insisted he had done. Letellier told the group that the bleeding in Joshua's brain was the result of "violent shaking or continuous hard hitting of the head as by an open hand." (In the late 1990s, the general public would come to know this condition in abused children by the label "shaken baby syndrome." Violent shaking of a baby or small child may cause the brain to reverberate within the skull. Blood vessels are torn from the brain, and the subsequent hemorrhaging results in brain damage or even death.) Letellier gave only a guarded prognosis for the boy's recovery.

Following these terrible revelations, Kemmeter contacted the juvenile court and once again the state took temporary physical custody of Joshua. She, along with the juvenile court intake worker and Winnebago County assistant corporate counsel John Bodnar, agreed that Randy would be allowed to visit his son in the hospital, but he would be permitted only to view him through the window in the intensive care unit. Kemmeter herself was allowed to see Joshua in the recovery room late that night. She noted extensive bruising on both thighs and two bruises on the upper left arm. He was on a respirator, and a tube drained fluid from the right side of his head.

With Joshua back in the state's custody, and the Oshkosh police undertaking a criminal investigation of both Randy and Marie, Kemmeter continued her role as family counselor. The following morning, she drove to the DeShaney home, where she found Randy resting on a couch. Marie was at a neighbor's. Still sensitive toward her client's emotional state (and perhaps fearing another violent outburst), she tactfully told Randy that, given the extensive machinery involved in Joshua's recovery from surgery, he should not enter the room but visit his son only through the window in the intensive care unit so as not to cause interference. But Kemmeter also wanted to know the truth about Joshua's injury. She had worked for more than a year to build a sense of trust with his father, and felt comfortable enough to put the question directly to him. "I asked Randy again what had happened the previous night," she later wrote, "explaining that I was not law enforcement." Interestingly, Kemmeter apparently believed that Randy would be likely to be more honest with her than he would with the police investigating the case. She counted on her image as a counselor and advocate, even distancing herself from the authority of the state. If, at this point, she held hopes that Randy would point to Marie as the one who had beaten Joshua, she was met with disappointment. He began repeating the story he had told the previous night, with some elaboration, about Joshua falling down the stairs. He said that he had been repairing a clock and, when the boy wanted to help, Randy had sent Joshua to the basement to get a hammer and screwdriver.

At that point in Randy's narrative, as recorded in Kemmeter's case notes, Marie returned and took up the story from him. The boy was wearing footed pajamas that were too big for him, she said, and while she and Randy were in the kitchen they heard him fall down the linoleum-covered stairs. "At no time did either one of them mention that they heard any screams from Joshua," Kemmeter later recorded, "just the bump, bump, bump." Kemmeter then asked Randy to continue the description rather than Marie. He said he found Joshua curled in a ball, unconscious, and carried him up the stairs; he was limp and Randy could not tell whether he was breathing. Joshua appeared to be gritting his teeth and blood was seeping from the corners of his mouth. Randy then pried his mouth open with a comb and tried to perform cardio-pulmonary resuscitation and yelled at the boy, attempting to wake him up. (It is likely that Randy had learned CPR during his service in the Air Force.) Getting no response, they decided to take him to the emergency room. Kemmeter did not record in her notes her own reaction upon hearing Randy's narrative, knowing that the medical evidence she had received from Letellier the night before indicated such a story was unlikely to be true. If she was disappointed, she nevertheless persisted in her therapeutic role as the DeShaney's caseworker, perhaps still believing that this violent and troubled family could be rehabilitated by the services of DSS. In retrospect, however, it is apparent that the social worker no longer had the ability to control the direction the case would take. Joshua's short life, already extensively entangled with the State of Wisconsin through its social service bureaucracy as well as its criminal justice system, was about to enter the public arena in yet another way.

On March 11, three days after Joshua's surgery, Kemmeter went to the Mercy hospital intensive care unit where she encountered Randy, Marie, and Rusty. Although Joshua had survived his surgery, she learned that the child's prognosis remained poor; the swelling in his brain had reached a dangerous level. At that point, Randy received a telephone call. It was Melody, Joshua's mother, calling from Wyoming. Kemmeter recorded in her notes that she had overheard Randy telling his former wife that the child had fallen down the stairs. Two days later Melody flew to Wisconsin, accompanied by her mother, Myrna Bridgewater. Both women met with the DSS child protective worker at Mercy hospital and were told about Joshua's trips to emergency rooms in Neenah and Oshkosh during the previous fourteen months. Later, Melody and her mother would allege that during this meeting Kemmeter said to them, "I knew one day the phone would ring and Joshua would be dead." Although Melody insisted that she could never forget the remark, Kemmeter herself always denied making it. Sometime over the next several days Melody sought out a lawyer to inquire about the possibility of regaining custody of her son. She did not yet comprehend that Joshua would never again be the child she had given up to his father more than two years earlier.

CHAPTER 2

Child Protection in the Nineteenth and Twentieth Centuries

In many ways, the sad story of Joshua DeShaney is a unique event, a confluence of factors particular to the individual personalities, family dynamics, community context, and historical period in which it occurred. Like any case that eventually finds its way before the U.S. Supreme Court, the case of *DeShaney v. Winnebago County Department of Social Services* began with actions and events initiated by and affecting individuals, a fact that is often obscured by the time the nine justices begin their review of the facts and the applicable laws and judicial precedents relating to the case. The legal system itself, through its rules and procedures — and the decisions of human actors within the system — shapes the contours of the narrative that is eventually brought for examination before the nation's High Court. In several critical ways, the Supreme Court case we know as *DeShaney v. Winnebago County* is a construction of the legal system and is not identical to the historical experience of the individual actors who are reflected in the official documents of the case.

In other important ways, however, Joshua's story is about more than the individuals involved; it is a result and a reflection of the larger historical processes in which it occurred, and therefore a full understanding of the case requires an examination of these processes. According to the National Center on Child Abuse and Neglect (located within the federal government's Department of Health and Human Services), Joshua's injuries at the hands of adults in his home occurred during a period in which reported cases of child abuse doubled, reaching 2 million by 1986 and 2.25 million in 1987. Even in the small city of Oshkosh, Wisconsin, Joshua was one of three abused children whose cases made local headlines in the spring of 1984. Just eleven days after Joshua's emergency neurosurgery, a three-year-old child was brought into the emergency room at Mercy hospital. Tragically, the little girl died as a result of the beating she had received from her mother's boyfriend. Another child, a twelve-year-old boy, was hospitalized because of the severe wounds he had received when his father had savagely beaten him with an extension cord. Douglas Besharov, a New York City prosecutor who founded the National Center on Child Abuse and Neglect (and later served as an expert witness in the civil lawsuit *DeShaney v. Winnebago County*), estimated that in the 1980s approximately one thousand children died each year as a result of maltreatment by their own parents. Further, the complex relationship between individual members of the DeShaney household and the personnel of Wisconsin's child protection apparatus, although in some senses a result of the fateful coming together of the unique personalities involved, nevertheless also reflected larger developments that had been taking place over the previous century.

The emergence of the state in child welfare work in the late nineteenth century (which included a wide range of activities concerning child labor, health, education, and recreation as well as child abuse and neglect), was inextricably linked to both the development of the social sciences and the professionalization of social work. In the Progressive Era (here defined as the period between 1880 and 1920), new research disciplines such as economics, sociology, and anthropology identified and explained social problems, and social work emerged as a new and distinct profession dedicated to implementing practical solutions for these societal ills. Child welfare activists along with other social reformers of the Progressive Era shared a preference for science over sentimentality, professionalism over charity, and systemic rationality over the particularity of human relations. They saw social problems as stemming from a corrosive environment resulting from rapid industrialization, urbanization, and immigration rather than the folly of individual human weakness, a hallmark of reform efforts in earlier eras. Strongly committed to the possibilities of human progress, they worked energetically for state laws, policies, and institutions to address the needs of children, the nation's future citizens and workers. The Wisconsin child protection system that the DeShaney family first encountered when Joshua was brought to the emergency room in January 1983 had its roots in the progressive movement. Wisconsin, in fact, had been a noted national leader in Progressive Era social reform.

In many respects, progressives' approach to child protection differed markedly from the efforts of an earlier generation of "child savers." Throughout the middle decades of the nineteenth century, attempts to eradicate domestic violence had been undertaken by private philanthropic and charity organizations often associated with evangelical Protestant churches. These local associations relied heavily on the volunteer activities of men and women who were deeply committed to reforming social ills but attempted no broader theoretical understanding of their causes. Child savers received little or no formal training for their vocation; they learned through their own trial-and-error experiences working among the poor and needy. For these middle-class Victorians, spiritual redemption and adherence to Protestant teachings was the key to a happy family, and material aid to troubled families often came with moral exhortations to live a more godly life. Jewish and Roman Catholic immigrant communities often developed an antipathy toward the Protestant "friendly visitors" who came to their homes urging spiritual redemption along with their offers of material aid. Beginning with the founding of the New York Society for the Prevention of Cruelty to Children in 1874, however, a more organized and secular child protection movement spread rapidly to other states as well as a number of western European nations. Although the various anticruelty societies remained private organizations, in many states they were granted the legal authority to remove abused and neglected children from their parents' homes and thus they worked closely and cooperatively with public and law enforcement agencies, so much so that the poor themselves often came to fear and resent them as much as they did the police.

Victorian Era child savers feared a future in which the ranks of the destitute and demoralized threatened to overpower the ability of social institutions to control them. Nineteenth-century benevolent efforts went hand-in-hand with the temperance movement, as activists soon identified — not incorrectly — alcohol abuse as a major contributing factor in family violence. Child protection workers understood "drunkenness" to be an individual moral failing rather than a medical disease; the modern terms "alcoholic" and "alcoholism" were virtually unknown to them. On the one hand, they characterized male drinkers as brutish and vile, rarely judging them worthy of sympathy or material aid. On the other hand, these Victorian moralists found it much easier to sympathize with female victims of domestic abuse at the hands of a drunken beast. Although middle-class child savers were generally harsh in their attitudes toward poor families, the absence of formal bureaucratic structures and rules for social welfare work also allowed a certain degree of personalized attention and individualized support for victims in domestic violence cases. Historian Linda Gordon's research in the records of the Massachusetts Society for the Prevention of Cruelty to Children, for example, demonstrates that child savers often devised creative solutions to their clients' problems; they were sometimes known to offer assistance from their own pocket-books. Therefore genuine sympathy as well as a desire for social control motivated nineteenth-century child protection workers. Gordon's research also reveals the degree to which social welfare clients actively shaped the outcome of reform efforts, assessing their own situations, weighing their options, and making use of the system of protective services in ways that best met their own needs. Female victims of male violence, for example, got the attention of welfare workers by reporting the abuse of the children in their households rather than their own at the hands of their husbands; these women understood that it was both safer and more effective to involve protection workers via the children rather than filing complaints against violent men on their own behalf. Despite the intentions of child savers, then, total social control was not possible when abused women asserted their own agency in this indirect way within the system.

Gender played a significant role in this history. Although, of course, both men and women are perpetrators of domestic violence, historically most victims have been women and children. Historian Elizabeth Pleck's study of anticruelty work in Pennsylvania and Illinois, for example, concluded that, although almost as many women as men were cited as abusers in agency case files, in 65 percent of these cases the women were acting in concert with men. Girls were as likely as boys to be victims of severe physical punishments, and girls accounted for virtually all reported victims of sexual abuse, their assailants including their fathers, stepfathers, uncles, brothers, and male boarders in the household. Gender also influenced how the problem of domestic abuse was perceived. For child protection workers, family violence resulted when households deviated from the ideal consisting of two married parents and their children; a man provided financial support, leadership, and loving discipline to his household and a woman nurtured and tended to members' physical, emotional, and spiritual needs — a full-time responsibility that precluded employment outside of the home. Gordon found that the records of the Massachusetts Society for the Prevention of Cruelty to Children contain many more cases of mothers deemed guilty of "negligence" rather than the physical abuse of their children. (It should be noted that the physical trauma of extreme negligence can be equally devastating for children; child protection workers regularly encountered lice and other insect infestations, malnutrition and other diseases, and loss of limbs through frostbite among the young neglect victims they assisted.) Further, "negligence" was a specifically gendered crime, as women were by Victorian cultural definitions solely responsible for the cleanliness, health, and behavior of their children; men could not be held negligent for infractions occurring outside their assumed sphere of obligation to their households. As Gordon's work also reveals, many poor and working-class women fell short of their own expectations in their roles as mothers as well; women heading households after the death or desertion of their husbands faced economic hardship and social disgrace as well as a loss of self-worth.

The stigmatization of the female-headed household was not, of course, unique to the Victorian Era; public blaming of single mothers for various social ills seems to be a constant theme in U.S. history. Family law scholar Martha Minow has observed that "mothers commonly have received blame for their children's situations, even when poverty, racial and ethnic status, or the woman's own battery at the hands of a man had more to do with the situation than did actions or inactions by the mothers." Ann Kemmeter, as we have seen, was inclined to suspect Marie, Joshua's caregiver and the single mother of Rusty, of abusing the child rather than suspecting his father. When Melody DeShaney surrendered custody of fourteen-month-old Joshua to her former husband and his new wife, she described herself as "too young, too poor, and too alone" to be an adequate mother. In 1989, the year the U.S. Supreme Court announced its opinion in Joshua's case, Kemmeter told a local newspaper that she had always regarded it as unusual that Melody had no contact with her son. "Mothers generally make themselves known," the social worker told the *Appleton Post-Crescent*. "I would say this would be unusual, for a mother not to have any contact." Although Randy DeShaney alone was convicted for the crime of abusing Joshua, neither Marie nor Melody escaped the publicly expressed censure of the DSS worker.

Females predominated among the ranks of Victorian Era child protection workers, although not among the organizational leadership. Elite and middle-class women found a natural niche in efforts to eradicate drunkenness and other personal vices as social expectations held them to be morally superior to men (and to poor and working-class women as well). Women's activities were framed in terms of their roles as guardians of the home and hearth. For the women who fanned out among the ranks of the poor and working class, combating moral pollution in their neighborhoods and communities was deemed essential to preserving the purity of their own homes. The Woman's Christian Temperance Union, founded in Cleveland, Ohio, in 1874, became the largest women's organization of the nineteenth century. Under the leadership of its second president, Frances Willard, the organization expanded its mission to embrace the cause of women's suffrage; Willard and other temperance leaders tied women's victimization at the hands of drunken and abusive men to their powerlessness in the political arena. Ironically, Victorian culture's emphasis on women as moral guardians of the domestic sphere, then, provided an opening for their participation in larger social and political causes, including the redefinition of domestic violence from a personal misfortune to a crime meriting prosecution and punishment by the state. Some scholars, including Barbara J. Nelson, have viewed this new activism on behalf of women's and children's rights as part of a wider interest in civil rights that blossomed in the post–Civil War Reconstruction and was manifested legally when Congress passed new federal civil rights legislation as well as the Thirteenth, Fourteenth, and Fifteenth Amendments to the Constitution.

Victorian social reformers associated community ills with the evils of industrial cities; by contrast, they idealized agrarian life as more conducive to individual well-being and household happiness. Thus, some child protection workers advocated changing troubled children's physical surroundings. In the mid-nineteenth century, the New York Children's Aid Society, under its energetic leader Charles Loring Brace, a Methodist minister, experimented with actually removing "street" children from inner cities and relocating them to live with rural families, where they often worked as servants in fields and farmhouses. Alternatively, children from households in which adults, through impoverishment, illness, or death, were no longer able to care for them were frequently sent by local courts to live in institutions and "orphan asylums" located on the outskirts of cities. Contrary to present-day assumptions, many children in institutions were not orphans at all; rather, they had been surrendered by a parent or parents unable to care for them at home. Many poor and working-class parents, in fact, viewed the institutionalization of their children as a last — and temporary — resort in hard times and voluntarily surrendered their custody. Both private and state-run institutions housed the children of the poor. To some extent, the romanticization of rural life is also a common theme in U.S. social and cultural history. The "nice kid life" Melody DeShaney envisioned for her son, for example, involved relocating him to a small town among the gentle rolling hills and lakes of central Wisconsin.

By the late nineteenth century, the Victorian model of child protection was receding in favor of the social welfare arena. As the new reformers of the Progressive Era came primarily from the ranks of the middle class and elite, they were much more likely to be college educated. A new generation of women emerged as the products of newly expanded opportunities for females in higher education; institutions for women's education commonly stressed social service as a responsibility of advanced education. Both male and female progressives overtly eschewed the personal style of earlier benevolent workers as "sentimental" and took care to eradicate any religious overtones from the "scientific" methods for advancing society's well-being they preferred. Using the new tools of social science, progressives examined the complex interrelationships among low-wage factory work, tenement housing, poor public health and hygiene conditions, and lack of education as they influenced families and households. Because they understood social problems to be systemic in origin, they often proposed broad solutions requiring the creation and active involvement of local, state, and even national government entities rather than the moral redemption of the individual. As political scientist Theda Skocpol, among others, has observed, progressive reformers linked state benefits to the poor and the working class to their vision of the welfare state, in which welfare provision was a public good rather than a matter of private charity. A healthy, educated, and stable citizenry, progressives argued, was vital to the reproduction of free, productive, and loyal generations of Americans.

Although they took pains to dissociate themselves from the ranks of Victorian Era "charity ladies," women in the progressive child welfare movement retained traditional notions about the inherent maternal instincts of women. As they maintained distinctly feminine identities, they claimed that an inherent proclivity for understanding and addressing the needs of the nation's most vulnerable populations gave them a rightful place in the arena of social activism. Historian Robyn Muncy has traced the development of a "female dominion" in social reform, an extensive network of women extending through local women's clubs to women workers' organizations to municipal- and state-run agencies. At the apex of this "female dominion" stood the U.S. Children's Bureau. Established in 1912 within the Department of Labor, the Children's Bureau was a federal agency dominated and led by women for several decades. Under its first chief, Julia Lathrop, the bureau launched an ambitious child welfare agenda that encompassed efforts to reduce infant and childhood mortality, prohibit child labor, expand compulsory public schooling, and promote recreation and leisure for children of the working class. Interestingly, preventing child abuse was not originally a stated aim of the agency, perhaps because that particular field became the purview of the newly emerging social work profession, as will be discussed later. Nevertheless, the bureau brought national attention to child welfare work; its programs and policies represented the institutionalization of many activities on behalf of children that had originated at the local and state levels throughout the country.

Kriste Lindenmeyer's history of the Children's Bureau reveals the ideological link its leaders forged between social welfare and the public good. The bureau's leaders cut their teeth on social reform through the settlement house movement. An idea borrowed from Toynbee Hall in London, settlement houses were small laboratories of the social sciences in which educated, middle-class workers lived communally in poor, usually immigrant, neighborhoods in industrial cities of the North and Midwest. Settlement workers studied the economic and social conditions of their neighborhoods, developing theories about the causes and consequences of urban problems. Settlement workers were distinct among progressive reformers, however, in the extent of their political and social activism; embracing the philosophy of pragmatism, settlement workers believed that theories were only valid if they led to the practical improvement of the human condition. Thus they inserted themselves into the political arena to a significant extent. The women who staffed and led the Children's Bureau, for example, not only identified the needs of the nation's children using the tools of social science but also organized to see that legal and political changes would address those needs. Programs to benefit mothers and children were not charity, they stressed; the building of the welfare state represented the means to a more just, democratic, and stable society. When the United States entered World War I, for example, bureau activists overtly linked the well-being of children to the war effort on the home front, encouraging local child welfare groups to infuse their efforts with a new patriotic zeal. Ensuring a future generation of healthy, educated, and well-adjusted soldiers, they proclaimed, was vital to the nation's military interests. As Lindenmeyer has argued, the activist women of the Children's Bureau constructed a discourse encompassing both social responsibility for children's needs and children's *rights* to have those needs met.

Settlement workers represented the most liberal and activist wing of progressive reform, but child welfare workers across the spectrum embraced the cause of women's suffrage. Like Frances Willard a generation earlier, they linked the deprivations faced by mothers and children to women's lack of political power in society at large. Their rhetoric extolled the social value of motherhood and sought public acknowledgment of women's work in raising future citizens and workers. Unlike a later generation of feminists, however, progressive reformers tended not to support married women's economic independence from men. An important exception was the movement for "mothers' pensions," advocated by progressives as a public entitlement in support of women's important work as mothers rather than a charity handout. Beginning with Illinois in 1911, a number of states established these benefit programs, in which certain women heading households received support from the state in order to keep their families intact. Wisconsin enacted a mothers' pension law in 1913; by 1919 thirty-nine states had established such legislation. Mothers' pensions were usually funded and administered by local government agencies, frequently by local courts, which were also charged with determining a woman's "fitness" to receive them. Widowed mothers of young children, for example, would typically be deemed worthy although women bearing children out of wedlock were not. The benefits were small and the procedures demeaning; nevertheless, mothers' pensions represented an acknowledgment of the social value of motherhood and, in many cases, spared women the loss of their children to institutions.

Despite their self-conscious efforts to represent a break from the Victorian past, progressives' own social vision, like that of their forebears, could also be flawed by a failure to acknowledge the salience of religious, ethnic, and socioeconomic class differences between themselves and the poor and working-class people whose lives they sought to benefit. Although collectively they championed a broad understanding of the causes of social problems, individual reformers could be rather oblivious to the exigencies of poverty, race, and illness affecting the people with whom they interacted in the mundane world. Reformers sometimes became exasperated when those on whose behalf they labored seemed too stubborn, feeble-minded, criminally inclined, or "foreign" to follow their guidance. If progressives advocated for the powerless, they nevertheless constituted a group apart. Gender could be a strong bridge between female reformers and the women whose lives they sought to make better, as in the case of maternal and child health programs and, to a lesser extent, organizations dedicated to improving wages and working conditions for women in factories and sweatshops. But class differences also lessened the effectiveness of many reform efforts, as did dissimilarities in religion, race, and ethnicity between reformers and their clients.

Although white ethnic immigrants in urban industrial cities benefitted from the progressive social welfare movement, they also developed their own extensive networks of cooperation and care, including insurance and "funeral" societies, for example, to help families cover the costs they faced upon the death of a relative. In the early twentieth century, the stark realities of racial segregation through both legal (de jure) and customary (de facto) channels meant that African Americans shouldered the responsibility of creating parallel structures of reform on their own, separate from those of white progressives. Further, scholars of the African American experience such as Darlene Clark Hines have noted that the overarching presence of racism — and indeed racial violence — in early twentieth-century U.S. society meant that middle-class reformers in the black community viewed themselves as occupying a status much closer to that of their poor and working-class clientele than did white reformers. The National Association of Colored Women's Clubs, which in the early twentieth century enjoyed a membership larger than either the Urban League or the National Association for the Advancement of Colored People, took as its motto the emblematic slogan, "Lifting as We Climb."

A new and distinct occupation, that of professional social work, emerged from within the broad paradigm of Progressive Era reform. Historian Daniel J. Walkowitz has identified one of the earliest uses of the term "social work" in an address by Mary E. Richmond of the Russell Sage Foundation at the 1897 National Conference of Charities and Corrections, an organization that in 1917 quite symbolically changed its own name to the National Association of Social Work. In the new paradigm of reform, social workers were to be the foot soldiers of the emerging welfare state. Removed from the higher echelons of politics and policymaking, social workers attended to the day-to-day demands of the newly emerging welfare apparati under construction at the local, state, and national levels. "Casework," the hallmark of the new profession, was modeled on the activities of the "visiting nurses" in large industrial cities who, beginning in the late nineteenth century, contacted poor and working-class clients in their homes to ensure that the services of the new public health system reached those in need of them. Like public health nurses, caseworkers had frequent contact with their clients in their own homes, and therefore they saw in a more direct and intimate way the myriad problems and needs of the poor. Also, like public health nurses, they were much more likely than other progressive reformers to note bruises, cuts, and burns on the bodies of women and children. The problem of domestic violence, they determined, was real and urgent.

But nurses had been perceived as low-status workers throughout most of the nineteenth century, associated with domestics such as maids, cooks, and nannies, and likewise the new occupation of social work carried a certain professional stigma. Social workers were also burdened by an association with the Victorian Era "friendly visitors" who had frequently frightened off the poor by arriving at their doorsteps unannounced. Progressive Era social workers were therefore eager to raise the status of their occupation and assert their value as educated professionals who performed their functions full time for pay. Colleges and universities established programs to train the new generation of social workers. The Chicago School of Civics and Philanthropy was founded in 1904, and in 1907 Simmons College opened its School of Social Work with support from Harvard University. The involvement of prestigious schools of higher learning provided a crucial means for social workers to raise their professional prestige. In 1917, Mary E. Richmond published *Social Casework*, a definitive text laying out the appropriate techniques of investigation, diagnosis, and response for social workers. Social work was now more clearly a distinct occupation within the developing welfare state, with its own functions, training, and methods. *Social Casework*, through a number of editions, remained the professional social worker's bible for decades.

As Walkowitz has shown, the profession of social work was significantly shaped by the progressive aim to rationalize and systematize the welfare state. Efficiency and standardization became important goals, modeled on Frederick Winslow Taylor's "scientific management" method for increasing industrial efficiency by standardizing the movements of factory workers. As social workers sought to distance themselves from the untrained and "sentimental" volunteer reformers of the Victorian past, the profession itself became increasingly bureaucratized and hierarchical. Standardized forms and a regimented lexicon (such as the one Kemmeter used to record her observations of the DeShaney family in her case notes) replaced the more impressionistic and idiosyncratic observations recorded by nineteenth-century child protection workers about the individuals and families they encountered. Walkowitz describes a day in the life of a "typical" caseworker of the 1920s, whose "work consisted of traveling about town, making arrangements for people, giving advice, providing referrals, and doing paperwork." She logged her day with items such as:

9:40 a.m.	At Main Office. Discuss relief eligibility of Mr. L. with Self-Support Department.
10:00 a.m.	Discussed with Home Economics department the

	possibility of sending child to camp for the summer.
10:45 a.m.	Visited lawyer to get legal aid for injured laundry driver.
12:00	Lunch.
12:45	E. 96th St. Convinces reluctant Mrs. C to lodge complaint against her husband.

As this evidence from Walkowitz illustrates, despite their efforts to raise the status of their occupation, social workers operated within a highly bureaucratic and rigid world. They had successfully shed the sentimentality and moralism of their nineteenth-century forebears, but at the cost of losing something of the idealistic and humane impulses that had undoubtedly inspired many social workers to enter the profession in the first place. Their job required formal education and training, but they lacked the autonomy and social authority of physicians, attorneys, and academics. As Walkowitz points out, it is perhaps not completely surprising, given women's historical economic status relative to that of men, that males did not flood the ranks of caseworkers; male social workers who failed to rise to the managerial ranks within an agency commonly left the profession entirely. Social work was, and is still today, a notably female-dominated field. According to federal census figures, women comprised 55.7 percent of social workers in 1910 and by 1930 made up 79 percent of the profession. The 1950s saw a slight decline in women's majority, down to 57 percent by 1960, but by 1970, around the time Kemmeter was entering the field, women's proportion had climbed back to 62.9 percent. Like most professionals, female social workers historically have received lower salaries than their male counterparts.

The onset of the Great Depression brought the needs of the poor — whose numbers were burgeoning — into stark relief. One after another, state-sponsored mothers' pension programs folded due to the combined blows of loss of revenue and skyrocketing numbers of families seeking aid; the Children's Bureau estimated that three times more families were eligible for mothers' pensions than were actually receiving them. Private charities, even those with decades of experience and community support, were overrun with families seeking relief. In June 1934, President Franklin Roosevelt established the

Committee on Economic Security (CES) to investigate federal policy and programmatic solutions to the crisis; in November, the CES expanded to include an Advisory Committee on Child Welfare. Its recommendations included a national program of aid to dependent children as well as federal funding for maternal and child health programs. According to historian Kriste Lindenmeyer, the CES also recommended federal funding for programs for children with "special needs," a category that included child victims of domestic violence. The CES plan for ensuring the welfare of the nation's children became part of the Social Security Act enacted by Congress and signed into law by President Roosevelt in 1935 (part of a package of economic legislation known as the New Deal). The Aid to Dependent Children program — which would popularly come to be understood as "welfare" — was added to the law in 1946.

New Deal social welfare programs built upon the extensive structures erected a generation earlier through the efforts of progressive reformers. Although provisions to address child abuse were included in the new legislation, Linda Gordon has observed that the nation's ongoing economic crisis generally shifted the attention of child protection workers away from problems of domestic violence, concentrating on child neglect among destitute families instead. As Gordon points out, the relative absence of physical abuse from public discussions of child welfare did not represent an actual decrease in its occurrence. Today, it is well established among child abuse experts that economic stress exacerbates family violence; under the dire circumstances of the Depression, there is no apparent reason to assume the incidence of physical abuse had in fact decreased. Nevertheless, the problem of family violence remained beneath the proverbial radar screen for both child welfare professionals and the general public for the next several decades.

When the issue of child abuse resurfaced in the early 1960s, it did so within a medical, rather than a social welfare, context. Scholars point to the publication of an article in the *Journal of the American Medical Association* in 1962 as a watershed event in the reawakening of the nation's attention to domestic violence. Interestingly, technology proved to be a major influence in this development. The authors of "The Battered Child Syndrome" gave this label to identifiable patterns of childhood injuries, such as distinctive bone fractures, that physicians could now detect using medical x-rays, and later, CAT scans (the technology used to identify Joshua DeShaney's extensive brain injuries resulting from several bouts of violent shaking).

The "medicalization" of child protection work had a number of important dimensions. First, it reflected the growing status and authority of physicians more generally in U.S. society, and more particularly in the area of child welfare. The Progressive Era child welfare movement had enlisted a wide range of professional and lay actors in the cause of improving children's lives. Progressive reformers had conceptualized social problems in broad, systemic strokes, and thus the solutions they proposed involved experts in a variety of fields. Children's health programs, for example, were as likely to be staffed by settlement workers as they were by physicians. By the 1950s, however, pediatrics had firmly established itself as a prominent specialty in U.S. medicine. Pediatricians, most of whom were in private practice rather than public service, replaced social reformers as national spokespeople for children's well-being. (Emblematically, in 1953 a considerably diminished U.S. Children's Bureau was subsumed under the Department of Health, Education, and Welfare.) With this transition to medicine came an emphasis on individual children's optimal physical growth as well as their normal cognitive and emotional development over demands for optimizing the economic and social circumstances in which all children were being raised. As a result, the new paradigm removed child welfare from the arena of politics and the discourse of children's — and women's — rights, where it remained largely dormant until the late 1980s.

Pediatricians were joined by their colleagues in psychiatry in the arena of child welfare, especially as it pertained to the problem of child abuse. Psychiatrists shared a growing influence and authority in American life with other medical doctors. Thus, efforts to prevent family violence increasingly entailed investigations into the psyches of adult abusers. The new focus eventually allowed valuable contributions to the field of child abuse prevention from both psychiatry and its cousin in the behavioral sciences, psychology. Linda Gordon's research in the case histories of the Massachusetts Society for the Prevention of Cruelty to Children, for example, reveals several interesting historical constants among child abusers that lend credence to present-day notions of a "cycle of violence" between generations.

Many child abusers were themselves abused as children, an experience engendering deep-seated feelings of powerlessness and self-loathing in victims. Adult assailants who terrorize those who are smaller and weaker nevertheless continue to see themselves as victims, often attributing outsized motives and disproportionate power to the children whom they assault. Gordon's historical evidence also supports psychological observations that abusive parents often carry inappropriate expectations of their children's physical, cognitive, and emotional maturity. But swinging the pendulum too far to the side of individual psychological explanations distracts from larger structural variables that also contribute to family violence. The stress of losing a job or a child's demanding and expensive illness, for example, can trigger an adult's sense of victimization and powerlessness, and in that distressed state he or she may be more likely to abuse a child.

Discussions about a new form of child abuse began to appear regularly in professional journals — emotional neglect. Social historians of the 1950s note the decade's seeming obsession with an extreme form of femininity in U.S. society and culture. During World War II, government propaganda had encouraged middle-class wives and mothers to leave their homes to take up vital work in war industries, and women answered the call in droves. With the return to peacetime, however, both popular and professional literature speculated about the fearful consequences of the major disruption that had taken place in thousands of U.S. households. An example of this discourse was the popular best-seller *Modern Woman: The Lost Sex*, published in 1947 by psychoanalyst Marynia Farnham and sociologist Ferdinand Lundberg, in which the authors theorized that women's independence from men during the war years had created a form of postwar neurosis in which women made themselves (and everyone around them) miserable by refusing to return to their appropriately submissive roles. Farnham and Lundberg anticipated an ensuing epidemic of family disruption, high rates of divorce, and skyrocketing juvenile delinquency in the postwar United States. Although these authors' views represent an extreme among the era's social scientists, nevertheless a new form of child abuse — emotional neglect — did appear on the radar screen of professionals in the human services.

Like physical neglect, emotional neglect was an infraction virtually unique to women, a dangerous departure from their roles as their families' physical nurturers and emotional caregivers. This discourse took place within a wider social context that placed unprecedented value on the nuclear family as the fundamental source of emotional and psychological fulfillment for all individuals. At the same time, however, popularized versions of Freud's "family romance" theories filled the pages of women's magazines and child-rearing advice manuals, warning women of the dangers of the "overbearing mother," especially focusing on the risk that such women would raise homosexual sons. (The American Psychiatric Association classified homosexuality as a mental disease until 1973.) From the perspective of social science and popular culture, at least, mothers appeared to be trapped in a no-win situation, capable of inflicting permanent grievous harm to their offsprings' psyches by being either too distant or too close to their children.

Social workers aligned themselves with the ascendant medical/psychological model of child welfare. Their training and expertise in casework — which, as we have seen, was itself rooted in the profession of public health nursing — put them in a natural position to make minute, direct, and particularistic observations about their clients' behavior. As mediators between troubled individuals and social services, they had long provided guidance and advice to families in need. They were trained to investigate and analyze myriad aspects of their clients' lives. The role of family therapist, then, was not too far a professional stretch for caseworkers. In 1960, the Child Welfare League of America published the first set of professional standards for child protective service workers, which became the generally accepted norms of the field.

By the 1970s, Daniel Walkowitz notes, the social work profession was increasingly split between therapist/caseworkers, usually signified by the attainment of a postgraduate degree such as a Master of Arts in Social Work, and lower-level employees performing more traditional, service-oriented casework in social welfare bureaucracies. A contemporary publication by the American Humane Association, *Child Abuse Legislation in the 1970s*, provides a succinct summary of the social work profession's view at the time Kemmeter was advancing her career by earning a postgraduate degree at the University of Wisconsin. The authors characterize the reliance on criminal prosecution for addressing the problem of child abuse as "a natural consequence [of] the desire to exact retribution" on the assailants of children. More preferable, they asserted, was social planning for the entire family. Child protective programs are "especially qualified to 'reach out' to families where children are neglected or abused. . . . The 'helping-through-social-services' philosophy is stretched to include the parents. This is based on the recognition that destructive parental behavior is symptomatic of deeper emotional problems. Rarely is child abuse the product of wanton, willful, or deliberate acts of cruelty. It results from emotional immaturity and from lack of capacity for coping with the pressures and tensions of modern living." The key to addressing domestic violence, then, was for the child protective worker to adopt the role of family counselor and therapist rather than an authoritative enforcer of the child protection laws.

Another crucial consequence of the "pediatric awakening" to the issue of child abuse — and evidence of doctors' influential position in American life — was the widespread public concern, and indeed alarm, over the problem of child abuse. Influential pediatricians suggested that child abuse was a prevalent problem that went largely undetected due to lack of training in how to spot the tell-tale physical and psychological symptoms for doctors, nurses, social workers, teachers, day-care providers, and others who dealt with children. The public became outraged by frequent and sensational stories of brutalized children that now appeared in the mass media. In response to public pressure, states in rapid succession passed mandatory reporting laws making it a crime for specified professionals to fail to report suspected cases of abuse. By 1967, just five years after the publication of "The Battered Child Syndrome," forty-four states had such laws on their books. The first federal law came with the passage by Congress of the Child Abuse Prevention and Treatment Act (CAPTA) of 1974, which provided more than $85 million in funding to states to develop programs for detecting and preventing child abuse and neglect, along with limited authority to experiment with treatments. Introduced by Senator Walter Mondale of Minnesota and passed easily through both houses of Congress, CAPTA also established a national data collection system requiring states to report certain data regarding child abuse and neglect and to enact statutes providing for the protective custody of abused children in accordance with federal standards. It was during this time that Wisconsin's system was established. In that state, a child protective caseworker filed a petition for removing a child from an abusive home with the juvenile court, thereby allowing the state to take temporary custody of the child without a formal termination of parental rights. In 1980, Congress followed up with the Adoption Assistance and Child Welfare Act, which, among other provisions, mandated that child welfare agencies make "reasonable efforts" to preserve family units before removing children from homes where child abuse was suspected (it was left to the individual states to determine the definition of "reasonable"), and required social workers to document their efforts toward this end in their written case plans. Kemmeter's case notes on her interactions with the DeShaney family (see Chapter One) reflect these federal reporting requirements. The 1980 law marked the first federal attempt to regulate child protective services in the United States.

The rapid succession of state and federal child abuse prevention legislation engendered a parallel rapid growth of bureaucracies for child protection within existing structures of social welfare provision. Kemmeter, for example, was employed as a specialized child protective worker within the larger agency of the Winnebago County Department of Social Services. (A 1999 report by Wisconsin's Department of Family Services noted that some seventy-one agencies in the state were involved in child protective services.) Significantly, as we have seen in Joshua DeShaney's case, the expansion of state child protection programs took place almost entirely outside of the criminal justice system. Unlike that of adults, children's safety was entrusted to social service providers rather than to the police. As historian Elizabeth Pleck has noted, these state-level child protective systems became large, lumbering bureaucracies riddled with the endemic social tensions the nation at large experienced over the rights of individuals, the sanctity of the private family, and the intrusion of the welfare state. Thus they became distinguished in the public eye from law enforcement agencies authoritatively investigating the victims and perpetrators of criminal behavior.

But, of course, children being abused in their own homes need a safe place to live. An initial consequence of the flurry of child abuse legislation and programs of the 1960s and 1970s was an increase in the number of children placed in foster care, which had evolved in all fifty states as an alternative to the institutionalization of children from abusive or neglectful homes. The number of children living in foster homes rose to 500,000 by 1977. After Congress passed the Adoption Assistance and Child Welfare Act to bolster the foster care system, states soon found that foster care systems were accompanied by their own problems. According to social welfare researchers Lela B. Costin, Howard Jacob Karger, and David Stoesz, state foster care systems were often poorly organized and haphazardly administered, prompting critics to doubt whether they could even be regarded as genuine systems at all. Horror stories began to emerge in the media of children becoming virtually "lost" in foster care bureaucracies, seeming to vanish from the oversight of overworked — or just plain careless — child protection workers. Further, emerging psychological evidence pointed to the trauma children — even abused children — experienced when they were separated from their siblings and parents. Foster children often lived in a kind of limbo, moving from family to family, with devastating emotional and psychological consequences, including the inability to form normal relationships with others and the perpetuation of patterns of abuse and neglect they had experienced themselves as children.

In addition, U.S. legal and social traditions made it difficult to permanently remove children from their parents' homes so that they could be eligible for permanent adoption by another family. As Costin, Karger, and Stoesz observe, critiques of foster care came from both ends of the political spectrum. Conservatives decried the growth of the welfare state as a dangerous intrusion into the rights of parents. In 1983, for example, sociologists Peter and Bridgitte Berger published an influential book, *The War over the Family*, a strong critique of social workers' alleged disempowerment of the poor through the undermining of their families, including the removal of children from their parents' homes. They criticized the growth in the size and authority of the welfare state since the New Deal as a dangerous usurpation of the rights of the private family. Among liberals, a backlash emerged against Senator Daniel Patrick Moynihan's report, issued a decade earlier under Lyndon Johnson's Great Society initiatives, that had posited a "culture of poverty" in which the children of the poor never learned to become economically self-sufficient and thus perpetuated welfare dependency across generations. In addition, racial tensions, violence in urban ghettoes, and the emergence of Black Power had significantly altered the trajectory of the civil rights movement by the 1970s. This shift brought forward a radical critique of the widespread institutional bias within social service bureaucracies that stigmatized poor African American families (many of which were female-headed) as deviant or unworthy simply because they did not reflect the middle-class, and largely white, ideal of a nuclear family. Racist white social workers, the new critics charged, ignored African American traditions of employing extended kin networks in raising children and labeled all female-headed households as inherently "dysfunctional" regardless of how well adjusted they actually may have been. Black nationalists as well as African American social workers denounced the practice employed in many states of removing black children from their homes and placing them with white foster families, labeling it nothing less than "cultural genocide." By 1983, after a decade of attacks from both ends of the political spectrum, the number of children in the foster care system had been cut in half.

Not of least importance in the growing critique of the foster care system was the fact that it was proving to be an expensive enterprise for states. Public outrage at child abusers was not accompanied by an equally enthusiastic opening of its pocketbooks to adequately staff and maintain quality alternative living arrangements for their young victims. In 1980, Ronald Reagan was elected to the presidency on a campaign to "get big government off our backs" and to lower taxpayers' contributions to social welfare. In 1981, Congress cut family welfare services (Title XX of the Adoption Assistance and Child Welfare Act) by 21 percent despite a significant increase in reported cases of child abuse and neglect. Political conservatives began arguing that federal interventions in family social services represented an intrusion on the rights of states to conduct their own programs in accordance with the needs of their own constituents. Religious conservatives expressed suspicion of anti–domestic violence activities that had emerged from the feminist movement of the 1970s, arguing that such programs undermined traditional patriarchal authority in the home and encouraged the breakup of nuclear families. Feminist activists stressed women's lack of economic independence from men as a crucial factor that entrapped women and their children in violent situations. They also pressed for the prosecution of violent husbands and fathers as criminals (see Chapter Three). "Discovering" child abuse, as it turned out, had been the easy part. Finding politically satisfactory, socially effective, long-term solutions for abused children would prove to be much harder.

The answer, or so it seemed at the time, was the adoption of the "family preservation" model, which became the standard for state child protection services by the time Joshua DeShaney first came to the attention of the Winnebago County DSS. Family preservation provided state-sponsored services to troubled families, offering support and keeping them intact. The journey Joshua's case took through the Winnebago County DSS in 1983 and 1984 was typical of the child protective system erected in all fifty states by that time. The state of Wisconsin placed responsibility for Joshua's safety in the hands of Kemmeter and the Winnebago County DSS, not the local police. At the same time, as a child protective worker Kemmeter operated within a paradigm of family preservation that stressed her involvement with the DeShaney family as a therapist and counselor rather than as a law enforcement official. Under this paradigm, the best protection for children was the *prevention* of domestic violence, and social workers could accomplish this not by removing children from the risks they faced, but rather by connecting their clients to a range of social services designed to shore up the family unit. Kemmeter's helping approach to her clients in the DeShaney household, therefore, clearly reflects her professional social work training in the 1970s. The field of social work did not begin to address systematically the dilemma of child protective workers' dual roles as therapist and legal authority until the 1990s, in no small measure due to the national notoriety *DeShaney v. Winnebago County Department of Social Services* brought to the problem.

When Joshua's case came before the nation's High Court in 1988, a public backlash against the family-preservation-at-all-costs policies states had adopted was just on the horizon. The previous year, a fifty-state survey conducted by the National Center on Child Abuse Prevention Research estimated that 1,132 deaths could be attributed to child abuse. Among the most outspoken critics was Douglas Besharov, who by this time had left the National Center on Child Abuse and Neglect to continue his work as a fellow at the American Enterprise Institute. Besharov argued that, although some families clearly benefitted from the therapeutic interventions of caseworkers, states' child protection bureaucracies were failing in their responsibility to children by persisting with hopeless cases. "There is such a thing as an appropriate time to give up on a parent," Besharov asserted in an interview in *Trial* magazine, a publication for the legal profession. When Joshua's case reached the Supreme Court, it came into the public spotlight in the wake of several sensational cases of child abuse resulting in severe harm or even death to the young victims, widely reported in the mass media.

The public outcry over the plight of abused children, although in many ways sincere and commendable, for the most part lacked a historical frame of reference for understanding the roots of the problem of family violence and the numerous and varied approaches taken to address it, with varying success, by previous generations. It is only relatively recently that scholars have begun reconstructing this history. This scholarship reveals the myriad and complicated interactions between private and public realms in child protection work, as well as between social reformers and those they sought to help. It also demonstrates the ambiguous approaches policy- and lawmakers have taken toward how best to remedy the problem. The American public abhors child abuse. But genuine concern for the plight of abused children has always been filtered through the prism of other values it holds dear, including the importance of the private family as the building block of U.S. society, citizens' rights to be protected from unwarranted government intrusion, and a limited — and inexpensive — welfare state.

CHAPTER 3

The Crime of Child Abuse

Although Joshua DeShaney was no stranger to the staff at the Mercy hospital emergency room, having been treated there for injuries on several previous occasions, his arrival on the evening of March 8, 1984, was decidedly different. This time Joshua was comatose, and a CAT scan revealed massive bleeding on the right side of his brain. B. F. Kayali, a pediatrician who initially examined Joshua in the emergency room, found the boy pale and barely breathing. His body did not respond to any external stimuli, including pain. Kayali contacted the hospital's neurosurgeon, Marc Letellier. That night, just two weeks shy of his fifth birthday, Joshua underwent emergency neurosurgery. For days afterward, as he lay unconscious in the intensive care unit, the prognosis for his recovery remained uncertain. Letellier had removed a large piece of the boy's skull in order to relieve the swelling in his brain, but the condition was not immediately halted. It would be some time before the medical staff attending him would be able to determine whether Joshua would live and, if he did, the extent and permanency of the damage to his brain.

The night of Joshua's surgery, Ann Kemmeter, the Winnebago County DSS child protective worker who had been called to Mercy hospital, telephoned the Oshkosh police. Over the previous months, Kemmeter had expressed in her case notes her concern about the possibility that Joshua was being abused in the DeShaney household, but she had not actually seen the child in four months. On this night, however, the physicians treating Joshua made it clear that they believed the child to have been deliberately brutalized. Responding to Kemmeter's call, Officer Scott Kronenwetter arrived at Mercy and spoke with an emergency room nurse who informed him about Joshua's injuries and the staff's suspicions. The DeShaneys were well known to the Oshkosh police, as patrol officers had been called to their home on numerous occasions over the previous months responding to complaints from neighbors about brawls between Randy and Marie. Apparently, there was friction between the DeShaneys and local law enforcement officers because, according to Kronenwetter, Randy refused to speak with him at the hospital. Kronenwetter had to call Detective Michael Novotny at his home in Oshkosh. A fourteen-year law enforcement veteran, Novotny arrived at Mercy at about 9 P.M. and was met by Kemmeter, who filled him in on her extensive involvement with the DeShaney family over the previous eighteen months. As a police detective, Novotny had not had contact with the DeShaneys previously, although he did think the name sounded familiar based on patrol officers' reports he had seen in the department. Kemmeter told him about the seriousness of Joshua's injuries this time, and relayed to the detective that the doctors gave the child only a 25 percent chance of surviving until morning. Novotny later recalled that the social worker's demeanor told him this was indeed a grave affair. The detective assumed he would be investigating a case of homicide.

Novotny could not see Joshua that evening in order to examine the child directly, so he began his investigation by questioning the emergency room staff about the nature and extent of the boy's injuries. A nurse told him about the multiple bruises on Joshua's entire body, most of which were old, but that fresh marks, deep purple in appearance, were on his face as well as his buttocks and upper thighs. She also said that tests had revealed blood in Joshua's urine, indicating internal bleeding. Kayali, the pediatrician, estimated that the deep purple bruising to the lower extremities was so extensive it covered from 50 to 75 percent of the surface area. He was convinced that the boy's severe injuries could not have been caused by a fall down the stairs, as Randy had asserted. He had confronted the boy's father with his doubts directly; Randy then admitted he had spanked Joshua earlier that day, adding that Joshua was a child "who needed to be disciplined." Kayali had found these statements incredible. He would later testify that, as a pediatrician, he had never seen injuries as alarming as those inflicted on Joshua's body that evening.

Novotny next interviewed Randy and Marie separately. Randy, who had arrived at the hospital in an extremely agitated state, had been sedated with Haldol at Kemmeter's request, and although Novotny found him surprisingly "mellow" given the stressful circumstances, he nevertheless evaluated Randy to be lucid, responsive, and quite capable of being interviewed. The detective took Randy's statement, in which Randy repeated the story he had told Kemmeter and the hospital staff that Joshua had fallen down the basement stairs at their home. He told Novotny that, when he could not get a response from the boy, he had slapped his face. The detective found it unusual that Randy said, "well, it was probably all my fault."

Novotny then spoke to Marie. He noted that she had stitches to her lip and damage across the bridge of her nose as well as what appeared to be a scar on one side of her face, apparently from an older injury. He thought she looked as if she had recently been struck hard in the face. Marie told the detective that "she believed that Joshua wanted to be hit so he did things to get spanked." Both she and Randy had frequent confrontations with Joshua, especially over the child soiling himself; they attempted to correct this by spanking the boy. Marie admitted that this happened on a weekly basis. After Novotny completed the interviews, Kemmeter gave him Joshua's DSS case file to review, including the records of his admission to the Theda Clark Regional Medical Center in Neenah and the child protective team's investigation of the DeShaneys the previous year. Novotny called Dee Dyer, the district attorney, to apprise him of the situation, and told him they might have a homicide on their hands. There was nothing else to be done that night, so the Oshkosh detective left the hospital. Novotny later recalled that he "got a sick feeling" from the case.

Joshua survived through the night, and the next morning Kemmeter contacted the juvenile court requesting authorization for DSS to take him into temporary custody. Now Joshua could not be removed from the hospital except by an order from the juvenile court. The Oshkosh police returned that afternoon to photograph Joshua, who remained unconscious and breathing through a respirator, several tubes draining fluid from the right side of his head, with nurses in constant attendance. Novotny noted the extensive bruising on both thighs and in the groin area the hospital staff had described to him. He was especially struck by two large bruises, one on each of Joshua's upper arms, which the detective later characterized as "distinct marks from where somebody grabbed him. . . . All the tell-tale signs [of abuse] were there." According to Novotny, such bruises tended to be left when a much larger adult grabbed a smaller person and shook him, or perhaps lifted him off of the ground.

The detective spoke to Letellier, the neurosurgeon, who told him that Joshua's brain trauma was inconsistent with a fall down the stairs. During the surgery, Letellier found that a significant number of blood vessels that were normally attached to the skull had torn away. He later testified in court that five or six groups of veins had detached, indicating that the child's head had been violently rocked back and forth many times. He differentiated what he had seen during Joshua's surgery from the more typical acceleration/deceleration brain injuries that occur to victims of car accidents in which a fast-moving vehicle comes to a sudden stop. In those cases, Letellier explained, a surgeon would expect to see only one group of veins detached because the snapping of the head back and forth had happened only one time. Thus, he had concluded that Joshua's injuries occurred when his head had been shaken violently several times. Further, Letellier said, he was suspicious because there were no skull fractures or fresh injuries to the *outside* of the head, which one would have expected had the child fallen down the stairs as the boy's father claimed. The doctor testified that he had confronted Randy with this evidence, and that Randy had become very angry, interrupting him and yelling, "What do you mean? He only fell down one step." On March 9, the critical point upon which Letellier and Novotny had come to agree was that Joshua had at some point been so violently shaken that he was now massively, and likely permanently, brain-damaged.

Novotny concluded that the severity of the boy's injuries required a physically strong perpetrator, and therefore he focused his investigation from this point forward on the boy's father. Randy was 5 feet 9 inches tall and weighed 155 pounds. Joshua was a rather slight boy for his age, weighing 39 pounds and standing just 40 inches tall, placing him at the fortieth percentile for weight but at less than the fifth percentile for height. (In other words, 60 percent of American four-year-old boys were heavier than Joshua, and 95 percent were taller.) Which criminal charges would be filed against Randy, however, depended on whether Joshua survived his injuries. Now that he had acquired more detailed information about Joshua's condition from Letellier, especially the surgeon's explanation of the torn blood vessels,

Novotny again spoke to Randy, this time advising him of his constitutional rights. Randy now admitted that he had shaken Joshua but insisted that it was only as an attempt to revive him because the boy had not been breathing when he found him at the foot of the basement stairs. He held out his arms and demonstrated to the detective a moderate rocking motion, indicating that he had done this in an attempt to awaken the unconscious child. Randy insisted that he had not shaken Joshua in a forceful or brutal manner. He wrote out a formal statement that included a description of how he had found Joshua unconscious, and had "held him by both arms and shook him and yelled 'Josh.'" The child wasn't breathing properly and his lips were turning purple, so he attempted CPR. When that proved ineffectual, he and Marie rushed Joshua to the emergency room.

Although Novotny was an experienced law enforcement officer, in 1984 police investigation of child abuse was a relatively new process in Winnebago County. The "rediscovery" of child abuse by physicians using medical evidence gathered by new technologies such as x-rays (see Chapter Two) had prompted states to revise their statutes during the 1960s and 1970s in order to designate violence against children as a specific crime, distinct from other forms of physical violence such as assault. Wisconsin law 940.201, "Abuse of Children," had been in effect since 1977. The statute defined "child" as a person under sixteen and specified that "whoever tortures a child or subjects a child to cruel maltreatment, including, but not limited to, severe bruising, lacerations, fractured bones, burns, internal injuries or any injury constituting great bodily harm . . . is guilty of a Class E felony" (subject to a fine of not more than $10,000 or a prison sentence of not more than two years, or both). Despite the new statutes, Novotny later recalled that not many law enforcement officers in the 1980s "had an inkling of how to deal with these things." The changing medical technologies employed in child abuse investigations required police officers to learn a great deal of new information about identifying the physical symptoms of abuse. "Pre-1980," he added, "if this would have happened, it would have been a fall down the steps, end of story." But times had clearly changed, and the public was now demanding that police departments devote more resources and care to the investigation of child abuse as a crime against the entire community, not solely as a problem within the private family.

Although physicians had been largely responsible for reawakening public interest in the problem of child abuse, the demand for changes in the prosecution of domestic violence as a crime had been spearheaded by feminist organizations beginning in the 1970s. In 1975, Susan Brownmiller's pathbreaking examination of rape, *Against Our Will*, served as a crucial milestone in bringing sexual assault out from behind the veil of secrecy where traditional societal norms had defined it as an individual woman's private shame. Feminist activists had pioneered the use of crisis centers and anonymous telephone hotlines for reporting and discussing rape and other acts of violence against women. They fought for the redefinition of rape and spousal abuse as criminal behavior, rather than as the inevitable, if unfortunate, consequences of male social and economic dominance, in families as well as within the community at large. As historian Linda Gordon has demonstrated, violent acts against women and children have integral histories, in perpetration as well as in the perceptions of the reformers who have sought to prevent these acts. Although both men and women perpetrate domestic violence, the overwhelming number of victims are women and children. Economically and socially dependent on men for their survival, women and children have lives and misfortunes that are historically intertwined. Thus, feminists' efforts to gain legal recognition of domestic violence as a crime encompassed children as well as their mothers.

The reawakening to the problem of child abuse in the early 1960s by pediatricians (see Chapter Two) also produced a proliferation of organizations dedicated to preventing child abuse that were not overtly identified with modern feminism. In 1978, for example, a nonprofit organization, the Wisconsin Committee to Prevent Child Abuse, formed with the mission of increasing public awareness about the problem in the state and "everyone's role in preventing it." The Milwaukee-based group, today called Prevent Child Abuse Wisconsin, also advocates strengthening public efforts and policies to keep child abuse and neglect from occurring, and has become part of a national network, Prevent Child Abuse America, founded in 1972. In 1979, President Jimmy Carter established an Office of Domestic Violence, beginning the federal government's official recognition of the extent of the problem in U.S. society as well as federal funding for the shared national goal of prevention.

But, to an extent, the increasing public cries for national attention to the problem of child abuse created tensions within the arenas of civil rights law and policymaking. On the one hand, a relatively small but distinctly vocal group of children's rights advocates pressed for the recognition of constitutional rights for children as separate from those of adults. These "children's liberationists" viewed children as another group in need of legal protection and political recognition; from this perspective, children were another "minority" to follow in the path blazed by the civil rights movement of the 1950s and 1960s as well as the emergence of modern feminism in the late 1960s and 1970s. Activists pushed for the protection of children's interests within the legal and social service systems and called for increased state services to safeguard children from abusive parents. On the other hand, civil liberties advocates feared unwarranted state intrusion into the privacy of the home and the autonomy of the family, especially regarding situations in which racial or ethnic minority parents faced punitive policies by local and state authorities. As historian Elizabeth Pleck has noted, the highly visible role of physicians in this period— professionals largely perceived by the public to be "disinterested" actors reporting "objective" medical evidence of child abuse in U.S. society—helped to ameliorate much of this tension. The authoritative voices of concerned pediatricians smoothed over many of the harshest criticisms of excessive governmental interference in the private family.

Occurring within this context of widespread public interest in the problem of child abuse, Joshua's tragic case quickly came to the attention of the local media in central Wisconsin. Novotny recalled that the case was a "big deal" for the city of Oshkosh. Yet, despite the national and statewide attention paid to the issue, the local public still found the case shocking. Accounts of Joshua's brutalization undoubtedly moved the citizens' sympathies, but there was an additional source of distress in the small Wisconsin city. Oshkosh residents were forced to come to the realization that their small community, surrounded by Wisconsin's gentle rolling hills, clear lakes, and dairy farms, was not insulated from the violence they usually associated with urban metropolises like Chicago to the south. "This is Winnebago County; we don't abuse our children here," was the way Novotny described the community's reaction.

Even more disturbing was the fact that within weeks the community learned of three separate cases of severe violence perpetrated against children, including the death of a three-year-old girl at the hands of her mother's boyfriend, Jeffrey Smolinsky, less than two weeks after Joshua's admission to Mercy hospital. The third incident, in nearby Menasha, involved a father's brutal beating of his twelve-year-old son with an extension cord. District Attorney Dyer commented on the unfortunate string of occurrences in the *Appleton Post-Crescent*, adding that although the cases were extremely troubling to his office, he could not attribute them to "any one thing" happening in the community at the time. Novotny recalled working the cases simultaneously, spending so much time on his investigations that he took to sleeping in his office rather than returning home in the evenings. It was, he said, a very stressful period, and the long hours he spent on the investigations took a temporary toll on his own family life as well. Nor was the community's apparent problem limited to these three highly visible cases. Within a few months of Joshua's final beating, the *Post-Crescent* reported that, in response to rising reports of child sexual abuse in the area, Winnebago County was forming a special task force to investigate the issue.

Joshua lingered at the intensive care unit at Mercy hospital for weeks. Novotny remained in close contact with Kemmeter, Dyer, and the juvenile court while the criminal investigation of Randy DeShaney continued. The detective was compiling evidence and interviewing neighbors, friends, and family members about the extensive violence that had taken place in the DeShaney home over the previous months. Police reports, of course, are not necessarily factual accounts; witnesses have their own motivations for shaping the events they relay to law enforcement officials, and they do not always recall events accurately even when they do intend to tell the truth. Details are often disputed by the various parties involved. Nevertheless, the fourteen-year veteran of law enforcement was thorough in his investigation, and the preponderance of witness statements he gathered indicated the DeShaney household was an extremely troubled place during the period from June 1983, when the family moved from Neenah to Oshkosh, to March 1984, when Joshua's final beating took place.

Some witnesses described Randy as a quick-tempered and even dangerous man. They relayed accounts of various acts of physical abuse they claimed to have seen Randy inflicting on his son, including kicking the boy while wearing boots and throwing him through the air on different occasions. At one point friends had become so concerned for Joshua's safety that they had actually taken photographs of his injuries, although they had never taken the step of reporting the abuse to the police. Some witnesses claimed that Joshua and Marie's son, Rusty, were hardly ever given food. By contrast, others were equally adamant that they had never seen Randy maltreat the children. They described him as a devoted and loving father and asserted that he and Joshua were very close. Randy, in fact, had been so concerned about his son's odd and difficult behavior that he had lost his job because he frequently left to go home and care for him. Some people insisted that Randy was covering for Marie's abuse of the children. Such positive views of Randy were not limited to his friends and family members: The dedicated and affectionate father who emerges from these witness statements is entirely in keeping with the artless, cooperative man who appears in the pages of Kemmeter's case file.

In stark contrast, other witnesses told Novotny that Marie was afraid of Randy because of his previous use of physical force against her and the children and was lying to protect herself from another beating. Marie told Novotny about incidents in which Randy had struck her, choked her, and given her black eyes. She claimed she had canceled job interviews because she had been too embarrassed to appear with cuts and bruises to her face. She said Randy became enraged at her if she stayed out late with friends or if she spent money. He also blamed her for Joshua's misbehavior but would threaten her if she tried to discipline the boy. One witness claimed that Randy himself once had admitted that he had a problem controlling his rage and needed professional help. Another feared that Randy would inflict harm in revenge if he knew the witness had spoken to the detective. In these accounts, Randy appears almost as a monster and Marie seems a distraught, quite unstable woman carrying deep emotional scars, apparently left by a difficult childhood.

At various times Randy and Marie accused each other of hurting Joshua; each adult admitted to hitting the other in various incidents. Randy had left Marie and the children numerous times over the previous months after bouts of domestic violence but always returned to the family within a few days. According to witnesses, the couple had once briefly separated following a particularly intense fight after which Randy received several stitches in his head (Marie admitted hitting him with a bottle) and Marie was treated for a broken nose. The brawl reportedly had ensued over Marie spending $20. Several witnesses claimed that heavy use of cocaine and alcohol played a significant role in the ongoing — and apparently escalating — physical confrontations between the couple. Drug abuse was also alleged in the depositions later taken in relation to the civil suit filed on Joshua's behalf. Marie herself admitted to Randy's lawyer that she was prone to drinking excessively and losing control of her anger. It was during these rages, she said, that she had called the police; she would not have done so, she told the attorney regretfully, had she been sober. As described below, Randy entered a drug treatment program as part of a plea bargain he reached with the district attorney's office. It should be noted, however, that neither Randy nor Marie was ever criminally charged with drug possession in relation to Joshua's case.

During their interviews with Novotny, both Randy and Marie also described ever more bizarre self-injurious behavior on the part of Joshua. Marie said that Joshua asked her to spank him at least once a week, and if she didn't he would proceed to harm himself. He threw temper tantrums, banged his head against the wall, held his breath until he passed out, bit his lip until it bled, and threatened to soil his pants. Significantly, their descriptions do not contain any expressions of sympathy that Joshua was enduring painful experiences or recognition that he needed help. Neither parent seemed to understand that his behavior may have indicated his distress at their own frequent loud and violent fighting and the instability of their home life. In reading their description in the police reports, one doesn't sense that the couple had any particular interest in understanding *why* the child acted up in such unusual ways. Joshua was by many accounts an intelligent, energetic, and assertive child; at three years of age his IQ had been measured in the "bright normal" range, and several witnesses — including Marie herself — told Novotny that he was a "very smart" boy. It is not unreasonable to surmise, therefore, that such a child would have been keenly aware of the turbulent dynamics in the household and acted out to express his fears or even to ensure his own self-preservation (for example, by demanding to be spanked as a way of exerting a modicum of control over the beatings, a syndrome identified by domestic violence experts among many victims of severe abuse).

But Joshua's behavior had only irritated and frustrated the adults responsible for him. At various times they attributed it to the boy being spoiled, or obstinate, or jealous of other children. They believed Joshua engaged in behavior deliberately calculated to make them angry in order to gain attention. At one point Randy also surmised that the child had learned this self-serving behavior from other children to whom he was exposed. Randy reiterated to Novotny, as he had asserted to the physicians in the emergency room and to Detective Nelson in Neenah, that Joshua was a child who needed to be spanked. Marie also said that the child was becoming increasingly "lazy," staying in bed until late in the morning. (This description is quite haunting given Letellier's view that Joshua probably experienced several brain hemorrhages prior to his final visit to the Mercy hospital emergency room. If this assessment was accurate, it would provide a reasonable medical explanation for the boy's increasing listlessness.) In the police reports the parents describe the four-year-old as willful and manipulative, even desirous of ruining their relationship as a couple. Marie alleged that the family had moved away from Neenah "for only one reason and that was basically because Josh wanted to move," a rather unusual attribution of power to a four-year-old child in itself, but also a statement that contradicted Randy's own explanation that he had thought it best to leave the town where his mother and ex-wife resided. The jarringly harsh descriptions of Joshua that Randy and Marie gave to Novotny seem contradictory to Kemmeter's assertions that Randy had been open and cooperative and very interested in learning how better to deal with the child. If Randy and Marie had received advice on parenting skills from the social worker, what they had learned is not reflected in the statements they gave to the Oshkosh police after Joshua's final beating. Instead, the detective's reports reflect a couple of adults seemingly rather determined to scapegoat Joshua as the primary culprit in the DeShaney's chaotic household.

Novotny's investigation uncovered evidence that Rusty, who was just two years old, was suffering physical abuse as well as Joshua, apparently perpetrated by both Randy and Marie. Witnesses alleged that the abuse had started when Rusty was only an infant, and that Randy and Marie each had at one time gravely endangered him. On April 26, 1984, the boy was removed from Marie's custody. The juvenile court determined that the toddler, like Joshua, was in need of the state's protection. "Taking into consideration Joshua's critical injuries, as well as the violence between the two adults in the home," Kemmeter wrote in the case file, "Dan Venne, Juvenile Court Intake Worker, Detective Novotny, and I felt that there was no option but to protect Rusty by placement in foster care." Marie was later reunited with her son, although it is unclear from the public record when or under what circumstances this reconciliation came about.

In her notes, Kemmeter seemed regretful that the drastic step of removing Rusty from the home had become necessary after all. Perhaps she was uncertain that the foster care system in Winnebago County would be able to meet the toddler's needs adequately. The DeShaney household had fallen apart violently and irrevocably, with two small boys as innocent casualties in the wake. The disintegration of the DeShaney family, and the tragic turn Joshua's life had taken, represented a professional failure for the child protective worker, and undoubtedly caused her great personal distress as well. Later, in a court deposition, the social worker said she was very fond of Joshua, explaining that she would hold the boy on her lap and read to him. Although her actions may have represented attempts to model appropriate parenting behavior to the adults in the home, it is clear that her interactions with Joshua had been pleasant for her, and they were certainly meaningful for the child. Marie told police that Joshua cried to go with Kemmeter when she left their home after her official visits, a pattern that apparently distressed Marie and caused her to become resentful of the social worker's interventions.

Yet, despite her stated fondness for Joshua, Kemmeter seemed to have been largely oblivious to the nightmarish picture of the household in which the boy lived, which was now emerging from Novotny's investigations. Just a few days previously, the child protective worker had visited the DeShaney home and by her own admission had noticed nothing amiss between Randy and Marie. Indeed, she had later recorded in her notes that she had found a "calm atmosphere" in the home, and she had believed the two were telling the truth when they told her they were getting along much better than they had been previously. She had even helped decorate Rusty's birthday cake the evening before Joshua's final beating. Publicly, Kemmeter insisted at the time that she had seen no "actionable" evidence that Joshua was in severe danger — a position she maintained throughout her career, in fact, until her retirement from the Winnebago County Department of Social Services in January 2005. Kemmeter's professional training in social work had emphasized the preservation of the family as the optimal goal of her efforts, and she had worked to build a trusting relationship with the DeShaneys. Although her case notes did eventually indicate her growing concerns that something seriously wrong was behind Joshua's frequent "accidents," nothing in her official accounts reveals her own personal reaction to the nightmarish reality of the DeShaney household.

It is rather unfortunate that, although the child protective worker undoubtedly grieved for the injured Joshua, her feelings are not apparent in the public record. Social work training in the 1970s, when Kemmeter had attended the University of Wisconsin, had instructed caseworkers to submerge their own emotional responses to domestic violence in order to ensure that the families continued to receive the help they needed. Social workers, one widely used textbook of the period asserted, "must 'manage' any bitter, shocked, or incredulous feelings about parents who hurt their children or who are indifferent to their distress or neglected condition. Management of such feelings includes keeping them subservient to the needs of the parents and the plan of treatment." Another text advocated that professionals encourage abusive parents to "develop a trusting dependence on the worker"; in order to build such trust, social workers should avoid "belittling criticisms and judgments" of their clients. Although one Supreme Court justice would later describe the social worker's notes as having an eerie, emotionally detached quality given the horrendous nature of the events she was relating in them, Kemmeter's rather stilted narratives reflect the social work profession's long-standing efforts to distance itself from the sentimentality of nineteenth-century child savers and establish legitimacy within the social sciences (see Chapter Two). Joshua's prognosis was severe, and his future very uncertain. The child protective worker still had much work to do regarding her young charge.

Interestingly, despite the severity of the violence perpetrated against Joshua by his father, Kemmeter retained her rather extraordinary concern and support for Randy, whom she also viewed as her client under the prevailing "family preservation" model that had dominated her social work training in the 1970s. Four months after Joshua's final beating, Kemmeter made the following observation in her notes: "During the course of Joshua's hospitalization at Mercy Medical Center, Randy spent the majority of his time, both day and night, at the hospital with Joshua. He did not interfere with Joshua's care — he was a very attentive father and very cooperative." She also noted, with a sympathetic tone, that Randy had become "very upset and angry of [sic] what he felt were accusations of child abuse against him" appearing in a story published in the *Appleton Post-Crescent*. (The story did not identify Joshua by name, but it did describe the child remaining in a coma following brain surgery and related that an investigation into possible child abuse was under way; in a small city such as Oshkosh, the DeShaneys' identities would have been rather easy to discern.) Staying true to her professional training, if Kemmeter did experience any revulsion or fury at Randy stemming from his brutalization of Joshua, or any sense of betrayal that the seemingly cooperative couple actually had been extremely deceitful, the social worker did not allow such personal reactions to surface in her records.

Meanwhile, it was becoming clearer that Joshua would, in fact, remain alive; he was moved from intensive care to the pediatric unit at Mercy hospital on March 30, three weeks after his emergency neurosurgery. Unfortunately, however, it was becoming equally clear that the injuries to the child's brain were as devastating as the physicians had originally feared. An electroencephalogram (EEG) revealed that the right hemisphere of his brain had been destroyed, leaving the left side of his body paralyzed. Letellier estimated Joshua had lost almost 40 percent of his total brain function. Joshua first opened his eyes on April 5, nearly a month after his surgery. One week later he could produce some vocal sounds and had regained his swallowing reflex. His body was also beginning to react to external stimuli. He could make some meaningful facial expressions such as showing displeasure when an ice cube was placed against his cheek or when his body was placed in certain positions he apparently found uncomfortable. But he also experienced frequent seizures during which he arched his back and stiffened his arms and legs uncontrollably. A consulting physician who examined Joshua at the request of Kayali and Letellier reported that the once bright five-year-old was now functioning roughly at the level of a seven-month-old infant.

On May 6, the juvenile court ordered Joshua to be transferred to a longer-term facility, the Central Wisconsin Center for the Developmentally Disabled in Madison, approximately 85 miles from Oshkosh. The following day a local attorney, Patrick Seubert, was appointed his guardian ad litem (a guardian for the purpose of legal proceedings). Joshua was moved to the center on June 5. In the intervening weeks, Letellier performed another surgery on Joshua to insert a metal plate in the child's head where a large portion of the skull had been removed in the previous operation. The new plate seemed to produce an improvement in Joshua's condition almost immediately, and it gave the members of the large medical and rehabilitation staff that now cared for him some reason for hope. Kemmeter continued to visit the child in Madison and to attend regular meetings regarding his status within the state social service system. Although he now had been relocated to Dane County for the extensive rehabilitative care he required, Joshua remained in the legal custody of the Winnebago County DSS. This was to be his status as long as the prognosis for his physical recovery remained uncertain and the criminal case against his father proceeded. As events transpired, it became Joshua's permanent status as well.

On May 30, two Oshkosh police officers arrested Randy. At about 6:30 that evening the police had been notified that a warrant had been issued by the Winnebago County sheriff's department. Randy was not at his house, however, so Scott Kronenwetter called Kemmeter, who told him that they probably could find Randy at his new job working as a security guard at an Oshkosh business. The officers then arrested Randy at his place of employment and brought him to the Winnebago County Jail. According to their report, the arrest took place on a public sidewalk outside Randy's place of employment; he agreed to go with the officers without incident. The charges listed on the warrant were two counts of felony child abuse and one count of conduct regardless of life as well as five counts of misdemeanor battery of Marie. Novotny later asserted that for a time during the investigation he thought there was enough evidence of Randy's intent to commit severe bodily harm to Joshua that he could have been prosecuted on a charge of attempted manslaughter, but the district attorney had not agreed. Eventually, the felony child abuse charges were dropped from two counts to one. (The misdemeanor battery charges eventually were dropped because Marie refused to cooperate with the district attorney's office, leaving them with no complaining witness.) During the bail hearing, Assistant District Attorney Eugene Bartman asked the judge to set the bond at $5,000, at which point, according to the hearing records, Randy reportedly became angry and lost his composure in the courtroom. Judge Carver set his bond at $3,000, and Randy, unable to come up with the money, was returned to the Winnebago County Jail.

A preliminary hearing in the criminal case against Randy was held on June 19. The local news media were there, and Randy's attorney Thomas Fink asked Judge Leo Mack to have them removed from the courtroom, without success. The court then heard testimony from Kayali and Letellier concerning the medical evidence supporting the charge that Joshua had been beaten on or around March 8, and that abuse likely had occurred over an extended period prior to that date as well. Novotny testified about his investigation of Randy, and a report from a psychologist who had evaluated Randy was also submitted for the court's review. It was the psychologist's opinion that Randy believed he was telling the truth about what had happened to Joshua on the evening of March 8. The court determined that, under the prevailing legal standard of probable cause, the prosecution had presented sufficient evidence that a crime had been committed against Joshua, and that the boy's father likely had been the perpetrator. Thus, a criminal trial would proceed. Randy maintained his innocence. His attorney held out hope that, were the trial delayed for several months, Joshua might recover sufficiently to be able to testify in his father's defense. He petitioned the court to release Randy from jail on a signature bond pending the trial date, arguing that Randy had not been able to see Joshua and this was causing him great psychological and emotional distress. The court granted the petition, and Randy was released on July 23.

The arrest at his workplace had caused his employers to fire him, so Randy spent the next several months supporting himself by working at odd jobs. In August, he filed a complaint with the Oshkosh Police Department against a friend of Marie's who had moved into his home while he was in jail. The woman had refused to pay rent, nor would she reimburse him for damage she had caused to the house, so Randy told her to leave. In his complaint, he alleged that the friend had returned and broken a window at the house. Two days later, Randy filed another complaint, this time accusing Marie of attacking him while she was in a drunken state, hitting and scratching him on the neck. He explained to the officer that he was worried his bond would be revoked if he got into any more trouble. The police officer suggested that Randy find another place to live, and also that he should avoid all further contact with his former girlfriend.

Meanwhile, it was becoming evident that, despite some initial optimism when Joshua was released from Mercy hospital, the boy was going to recover only very incrementally, and then only after many months, and probably years, of intensive therapeutic services. A CAT scan taken in July showed virtually no changes in the condition of his brain. The left side of his body remained paralyzed, and he continued to experience frequent seizures. He could, however, make eye contact with his therapists and would put toys placed in his right hand into his mouth as a way to explore them, in the manner of a baby. In August, Joshua was transferred from the facility in Madison to the Gillette Children's Hospital in St. Paul, Minnesota. Judge Robert Hawley was unwilling to delay Randy's trial indefinitely while they waited for Joshua to recover, so he made an inquiry to Linda Krach, a physician at the Gillette Center, concerning her prognosis for the boy. On September 11, Krach replied that Joshua would never be able to testify in court, even in the unlikely event that he could remember the incident of six months earlier at all. The child could neither talk nor follow verbal commands. After months of intensive physical and occupational therapy, Joshua was now able to smile and was slowly regaining some degree of muscle tone on the right side of his body. He continued to put toys in his mouth, but sometimes he could touch them with the index finger of his right hand. (The left side of his body remained paralyzed.) The child, then, had made some small improvements in his motor abilities. However, given the extent of the brain injury he had sustained, Krach did not expect further significant functional improvements in Joshua's condition. It was a bleak picture of the five-year-old's future.

It was a stark picture for Randy's criminal defense as well. If he had held out hope that his son would someday attest to his innocence, it had become apparent that Joshua would probably never recover to such an extent that he would be able to do so. Of course, it is entirely possible that Randy was telling the truth and Joshua actually had fallen down the stairs accidentally in the DeShaney home that evening. Letellier's description of the boy's numerous head injuries suggests the possibility that Joshua was already losing control of his motor abilities before his final trip to the emergency room, and therefore slipping, falling, and fainting seemingly "for no reason" could have been the result. Letellier's testimony, however, also indicates that such a fall down the basement stairs as described by Randy and Marie was extremely unlikely to have been the cause of the severe damage to the boy's brain; that trauma had a completely different origin, the result of bleeding from repeated, violent shaking. Regardless of the specific scenario in which Joshua became comatose, the state had constructed a strong evidentiary case against his father. The expert testimony of Kayali and Letellier had been devastating. Novotny later recalled that the photographs taken of Joshua in Mercy hospital by the Oshkosh police were extremely damaging as well. His own succinct summary of the case was, "Marie's not talking, Randy talked a little bit, but the injuries speak for themselves." Under the circumstances, Randy and his attorney, Fink, agreed to a plea bargain.

On December 10, 1984, Randy entered an "Alford plea," an arrangement by which he did not admit to being guilty of the two felony charges against him but was making a "voluntary, knowing, and intelligent choice" that pleading "no contest" was his best option, given the strength of the prosecution's case. In doing so, Randy waived certain constitutional rights, such as the Fifth Amendment's protection against self-incrimination, the Sixth Amendment's right to confront the witnesses against him, and the Seventh Amendment's right to a trial by jury. In return, the state amended the count of injury by conduct regardless to life to felony battery; the single count of felony child abuse remained as originally charged. Randy's Alford plea relieved the state of the legal burden to prove his guilt "beyond a reasonable doubt." Novotny later expressed the belief that there was some pressure to settle the case because the district attorney's office was very busy preparing for the manslaughter trial of Jeffrey Smolinsky at the same time. (A jury found Smolinsky guilty of second-degree murder for the death of his girlfriend's three-year-old child on February 19, 1985. Interestingly, Smolinsky had pleaded innocent to the charge, claiming that the little girl had fallen down the stairs.) The Oshkosh detective also admitted to being somewhat disappointed that the state had made the deal with Randy DeShaney; he would have preferred a stiffer sentence.

Randy's sentencing hearing was held on February 6, 1984, eleven months after Joshua's final beating. Randy appeared in Judge Hawley's courtroom along with his lawyer. Marie was also present, apparently to provide moral support to Randy as he faced his sentence. Assistant District Attorney Bartman asked the court to impose the maximum sentences, given the extent and severity of Joshua's injuries. He also asserted that evidence presented to the court had shown Randy to have extreme difficulty controlling his anger, and therefore he represented a danger to the community. For his client's part, Fink reminded the court that Randy had no prior criminal or juvenile records and that he was a four-year veteran of the U.S. Air Force and had been honorably discharged. The attorney believed that the picture the district attorney had presented of Randy's tendency toward violent behavior had been distorted. Marie had admitted to him she had called the police several times only because she had been angry and drunk; she insisted she would not have done so had she "had her wits about her at the time." Fink also stated his objections to the district attorney's entire approach to Randy's prosecution. Since no one actually knew what had happened to Joshua on March 8, he alleged, the district attorney had merely "taken a poll" to see if Randy were *capable* of beating a child and, upon learning that he was *capable*, had prosecuted him as if he *had* done so. He asked the court to allow Randy to serve the sentences for the two charges concurrently, each of which carried a maximum penalty of two years in prison. If the court's point was to "teach Randy a lesson," Fink insisted, then "two years will accomplish that." When asked whether he had anything to say to the court, Randy replied, "no sir." Those were his only words recorded at the time of his sentencing.

But Judge Hawley was not convinced by Fink's arguments. The court, he said, "would not close its eyes" to the significant medical evidence that Joshua had suffered repeated abuse at the hands of his father, over an extended period of time, acts that the judge found "just reprehensible." He took note of the testimony attesting to Joshua's present condition, citing specifically a report from the Gillette Children's Hospital that because he was virtually totally immobile, Joshua was being fit with a special wheelchair with upholstered inserts and shoulder supports to allow him to sit upright. "In my mind," Judge Hawley said, "this little boy's life has been decreased accordingly that some might even argue even if he has a life or existence of his own anymore; whether he will ever be able to enjoy anything of his life or of this world." He was, he added, sorry that Randy had not accepted the help he had been offered over the previous two years by Kemmeter and the Winnebago County DSS "so this could have been prevented somehow." Accordingly, Hawley sentenced Randy to the maximum penalty of two years for each of the counts — four years to be served consecutively — asserting that "it would unduly depreciate the seriousness of the offenses" if the court did not impose the maximum sentence the law allowed.

On February 14, 1985, Randy DeShaney entered the Dodge Correctional Institution in Waupun, Wisconsin, a little more than 30 miles north of Oshkosh. He was paroled two years and seven months later and served the remainder of his sentence in an area drug treatment facility. He has no subsequent criminal record in the state of Wisconsin.

DeShaney v. Winnebago County
in the Lower Courts

In early October 1985, nineteen months after his traumatic brain injury, Joshua's recovery remained slow and uncertain. Now six years old, he had received rehabilitation services at the Central Wisconsin Center for the Developmentally Disabled in Madison and spent several months at the Gillette Children's Hospital in St. Paul, Minnesota. He had undergone additional surgery. In the fall of 1984 he had been placed with a foster family and continued to receive the services of several rehabilitation professionals and physicians through the Marshfield Clinic in Marshfield, Wisconsin. Unfortunately, however, after more than a year Joshua had not exhibited much improvement, and in fact appeared to be deteriorating. Joshua's foster parents became concerned that he seemed to be experiencing some regression in controlling his head and body, and had been refusing to eat as well as having difficulty digesting food. Stephen Wagner, Joshua's pediatrician at the Marshfield Clinic, had raised the possibility of inserting a feeding tube. Although he could not speak, he appeared to be experiencing pain when he was put through physical therapy exercises. The foster parents came to believe that, despite the many hours of care they had given Joshua, he had shown no progress and, because they were responsible for other children as well, they would no longer be able to provide for him. They put in a request to the Winnebago County Department of Social Services, which continued to have legal custody of the child, to have Joshua transferred out of their home. On October 8, 1985, Lori Dickman, a social worker with DSS, wrote to Melody DeShaney in Cheyenne updating her on her son's condition and informing her that the department was looking for a qualified foster home to which he could be moved. Eventually, Joshua was placed in another foster home in Oshkosh that specialized in children with disabilities.

By now it was more than clear to Melody that Joshua needed a great deal of specialized care, and that he would need it for the rest of his life. It was equally apparent that this care would be astronomically expensive, and that she had no way to pay for it. Within a few days of Joshua's surgery, she had begun to look into the possibility of regaining legal custody of her son, and had contacted a local attorney in Oshkosh. Initially she had wanted to move Joshua to a facility in Cheyenne so the child could be near her and her own mother. But it soon became evident that the cost of such a plan would be prohibitive given her means, as she worked in low-paying jobs and lacked medical insurance benefits. Detective Novotny later recalled Melody coming to see him at the Oshkosh police station and asking him to tell her exactly what had happened to Joshua. The detective told her he was "one hundred percent sure" that Randy, her former husband, had abused her son. The picture he presented that day was a far cry from the "nice kid life" Melody had expected for Joshua when she had surrendered him to the legal custody of his father more than two years earlier.

Uncertain about her options, upon her return home she looked in the telephone book for names of attorneys in Cheyenne who practiced in the area of personal injury law. She found Donald J. Sullivan, a specialist in health care and medical malpractice as well as personal injury. Sullivan had received a juris doctorate from Syracuse University in 1970. An experienced trial attorney, he had been active in the legal profession for fifteen years, and had served for one year in the county government of Onandaga County, New York, before taking his family to Wyoming. Although he had lived in the East since he was a young child, Sullivan later explained, he and his wife had decided that Cheyenne would be a good place to raise their children — ironically, a sentiment not so very different than Melody's own thoughts when she had surrendered custody of Joshua to live with his father in central Wisconsin.

Sullivan was extremely moved by the story Melody DeShaney told him when she met him at his Cheyenne office. "It only takes two minutes," he later asserted, "to figure out that this is a tragic story, and an outrage." Melody told him that, despite Joshua's frequent trips to the emergency room and Ann Kemmeter's growing suspicions about violence in the DeShaney household, no one from Winnebago County DSS had ever attempted to contact her. She maintained that her own attempts to call Joshua had been consistently stymied by the DeShaney family and, in the absence of knowledge to the contrary, she had assumed that her son was doing well. She was haunted by her recollection of Kemmeter's statement the night she arrived at the hospital in Oshkosh: "I always knew one day the phone would ring and Joshua would be dead." She described to Sullivan the severity of Joshua's injuries, explaining that, although his prognosis remained uncertain, there was at least a chance that with high quality rehabilitative care he could improve.

Sullivan looked into Melody's legal options, initially investigating a "garden variety negligence" suit in state court in Wisconsin against the Winnebago County DSS. He felt confident that, under the laws of Wisconsin, Melody could win such a suit. His research also revealed, however, that under that state's tort law any damage award she might win would be limited to just $50,000 total; at Joshua's current level of care, Sullivan estimated that the costs would amount to approximately $60,000 *per year.* A federal lawsuit, however, offered the chance to collect a much higher dollar amount in damages. Sullivan presented Melody with a choice: She could file a suit in state court, which she would probably win although the award would be of very little actual use to Joshua, or she could file a federal lawsuit, which would be much harder to win but held out the potential to make a real difference in her child's life.

Melody weighed the options. She had spent more than a year telling herself that, somehow, she "should have known" that her son had been trapped in a violent home more than a thousand miles away; the public record reveals that she sought counseling from a therapist in Cheyenne to help her cope with the grief and depression she felt over Joshua's tragedy. Later, as she waited for *DeShaney v. Winnebago County* to be heard by the nine justices of the U.S. Supreme Court, she would tell William Glaberson of the *New York Times* that, although Joshua no longer knew who she was, she came to think of taking legal action as "a little bit of a healing process to be able to fight back. At least you know you're doing something." In April 1985 Melody and Joshua filed a federal suit in the U.S. District Court in Milwaukee, Wisconsin. The suit named as its defendants the Winnebago County DSS, Ann Kemmeter and Cheryl Stelse, and the director of social services for the State of Wisconsin, Linda Reivetz.

(Randy DeShaney, who went to prison after pleading no contest to criminal charges related to his beating of Joshua, was originally included as a defendant in the civil suit, but was dropped when the case went to the U.S. Court of Appeals.)

The strategy Sullivan developed was composed of two separate parts: establishing that the tort of negligence had occurred, and establishing that it was a violation of Joshua's constitutional rights. The first half of Sullivan's strategy was rooted in three principles arising from the common law of negligent and intentional torts. The first principle involves the most basic definition of "negligence." According to *Black's Law Dictionary*, negligence is a "failure to exercise a standard of care that a reasonably prudent person would have exercised in a similar situation." To prove negligence, Sullivan would have to convince the court that, by not removing Joshua from his father's home despite signs he was being abused there, the defendants had failed to meet a standard of care recognized by both the social work profession in general and by the State of Wisconsin through its delegation of the authority to DSS agents to remove children from such a home.

"Negligence," however, does not take place in a vacuum; like many legal definitions, it is a relational term that involves the entire context in which the act takes place. The second principle, then, deals with the *result* of a negligent act. In an opinion foundational to modern U.S. tort law, *Palsgraf v. the Long Island Railroad Company*, Supreme Court Justice Benjamin Cardozo established a sort of chain reaction of cause-and-effect factors that determined whether an act of negligence could be considered actionable (fitting the criteria for a lawsuit): "Negligence is not a tort unless it results in the commission of a wrong," the justice wrote in 1928, "and the commission of a wrong imports the violation of a right, in this case [Palsgraf's lawsuit], we are told, the right to be protected against interference with one's bodily security." But, he reminded the Court, "bodily security is protected, not against all forms of interference or aggression, but only against some." Unintended accidents, for example, are not necessarily actionable wrongs, even if they result in physical injuries. Therefore, a person seeking a legal remedy for bodily harm needed to do more than merely demonstrate that the damage happened. "If the harm was not willful," Cardozo wrote, "he must show that the act as to him had possibilities of dangers so many and apparent as to entitle him to be protected against the doing of it though the harm was unintended." Based on this second principle, Sullivan would argue that, even if the defendants had not willfully harmed Joshua, they were still negligent because their failure to remove him from his father's violent home had resulted in dangers "many and apparent" to the boy.

The first two principles described above, however, evolved from cases involving negligent acts committed by one private party upon another. Under general legal principles, states are not held liable for harm inflicted upon an individual by a third party. Therefore, Sullivan had to rely on a third principle of tort law to make Joshua's case, that of "special relationships." Under the "special relationship" theory, a state may assume an affirmative duty to protect an individual from harm done by a private party if the state has placed the individual in a situation in which he cannot defend himself. In the fifteen years preceding Joshua's case, the federal courts had recognized the existence of a special relationship — and therefore conferred on the states an affirmative duty to protect it — in cases in which police left children stranded in an automobile on a highway after arresting their mother (*White v. Rochford*), when prison guards knowingly exposed an inmate to a risk of assault (*Spence v. Staras*), when a patient in a mental hospital was assaulted by his fellow patients (*Youngberg v. Romeo*), and when prison officials deliberately denied an inmate urgently needed medical treatment (*Benson v. Cady*).

Joshua DeShaney, of course, was not confined within the walls of a state institution when he received the blows from his father, nor had he been placed in the Wisconsin foster care system. Sullivan's task, therefore, was to convince the court that his case was nevertheless sufficiently similar to the other recent federal court cases to warrant applicable rulings. Joshua lived in Wisconsin, where, by statute, he was dependent on the state's child protective system to safeguard him from his father's beating. Although the Wyoming court had granted Randy legal guardianship of his son, the guardian himself had now become a threat to the boy. Joshua could not depend on his father to protect him. Nor could the child turn to the police as could an adult in a domestic violence situation. As legal scholar Laura Oren has observed, the law treats abused children differently than adults in need of physical protection because "their fate is not in the hands of the police," but rather in the hands of specialized state agents in child welfare agencies. Sullivan argued that the state had organized a child protective system in which only the system itself could have protected Joshua — not his father and not the police — and thus the state had acquired an affirmative duty to protect him. He tried to convince the court that, although Joshua was not living in a brick-and-mortar state institution, the theory of special relationships nevertheless applied to his case because the state had constructed what was, in essence, a virtual institution in which Joshua was confined. Because the state had placed Joshua in this virtual institution, it had acquired an affirmative duty to protect him while he was living in it. And, because the Winnebago County DSS failed to protect Joshua from his father's violence, the defendants were liable. To make this case, Sullivan needed to paint an exhaustively detailed picture describing the extensive involvement the DSS, particularly Ann Kemmeter, had with the DeShaneys over a period of fourteen months, the degree of awareness the defendants had that Joshua was being abused in his home, and the nature of the boy's injuries, including the medical evidence that they had collected over a period of months prior to his final beating.

The second part of Sullivan's strategy involved establishing the basis by which Joshua's case could be brought to federal rather than state court. Justice Cardozo's chain of reasoning had also required that, if a claim were brought in federal court, the act of negligence had to have resulted in a violation of a person's rights under the U.S. Constitution, specifically the right to bodily security. (The section of the U.S. Code that allows citizens to bring civil lawsuits to federal court when they believe their constitutional rights have been violated is 42 U.S.C. 1983.) The question of whether individuals enjoy a constitutional right to protect their own bodies, however, is a complex matter in U.S. law; not all claims for bodily security have been recognized by the Supreme Court. The Court, for example, has upheld state public health laws requiring citizens to be vaccinated against smallpox or face a penalty even if individuals believed that the procedure would make them sick or kill them (*Jacobson v. Massachusetts*, 1905). The Court also allowed to stand state eugenic statutes mandating the compulsory sterilization of certain persons whose sexual reproduction was deemed to be a threat to a community's health and welfare, such as those believed to be carrying heritable traits for criminality or imbecility (*Buck v. Bell*,

1927). Historically, several groups of people did not possess the right to determine what happened to their own bodies at all. Slaves, for example, had been considered the chattel property of their owners and therefore enjoyed no protections for bodily security under the law. And, under the common law doctrine of "coverture," in which a married women's legal identity was subsumed under that of her husband, wives did not possess a right to bodily self-determination. The law regarded a husband's sexual access to his wife's body as his marital privilege, and physical "discipline" by a husband of his wife (to a point) had also been recognized as a man's legal right. Indeed, the law had expected male heads of households to retain discipline and order in their own "little commonwealths" as their obligation to the community's safety and well-being. The precise nature of the right to bodily security, then, had been subject to varying interpretations, both over time and among groups of individuals.

As the legal, social, and economic dependents of their parents, children exercised little or no legal autonomy, bodily or otherwise. Although the 1960s and 1970s had seen a flurry of state and federal legislation regarding the prevention of child abuse (see Chapter Two), children still occupied a legal status very different from that of adults. And, as we have seen, in the 1980s the field of social work had come to be dominated by the "family preservation" model in which the caseworker acted as an advocate and counselor to the entire household. Under this system, the child protective worker did not represent a child's interests against those of his or her parents; social workers, in fact, strove to keep the family together if at all possible and to connect them to state social services for the purpose of supporting the family as a unit. Kemmeter's case notes reveal the ways in which she regarded Randy DeShaney as her client as well as Joshua, and persisted in trying to help him even when it became apparent that Joshua had been brutally beaten. Thus, children suffering from abuse and neglect at the hands of their parents or legal guardians inhabited a peculiar status in which their physical safety depended on state agents whose goal was not to penalize offending parents (indeed, as we have seen, a "punitive attitude" on the part of caseworkers toward their clients was discouraged in professional social work training), but rather to ameliorate the family's environmental circumstances so that adults would cease maltreating their children. The second part of

Sullivan's strategy, then, required the court to recognize children's right to bodily security *separate and apart* from the long-established rights of their parents to discipline and control their offspring.

Sullivan grounded this claim in the Fourteenth Amendment; specifically, its provision to provide federal safeguards for citizens' rights to life, liberty, and property against state infringement without due process of law. Sullivan needed to convince the court that Joshua's injuries at the hands of his father constituted a violation of his rights to life (the life he had enjoyed as a bright, healthy four-year-old boy before he had become permanently paralyzed and severely brain-damaged) as well as to liberty (the freedom to move about physically and to exercise autonomy when he reached adulthood). The State of Wisconsin, his argument would insist, had violated these rights through the actions of its agents in the Winnebago County DSS. It was an ambitious argument, one that asked the court to expand the universe of constitutional civil rights protections to include a child's right to be protected from his parents' abuse. It also required the court to accept the notion that the state's failure to protect Joshua — action it had *not* done — was equivalent to the state *taking action* in violation of his rights, as the text of the Fourteenth Amendment reads. Thus, the personal injury attorney was venturing out in a way that, although not completely unproven, nevertheless did suggest a departure from the mainstream of Fourteenth Amendment jurisprudence. He was well aware of the potential of this case to make a significant impact in civil rights law.

Because the case was filed in the U.S. District Court in Milwaukee, the Cheyenne-based attorney needed to obtain local counsel to join him in the case. Through his involvement with the Trial Lawyers' Association (Sullivan served as president of this organization in 1986), he was referred to Curry First, a noted civil rights attorney who was also the litigation director for the Legal Aid Society of Milwaukee. First, a 1968 graduate of Vanderbilt Law School, had been practicing civil rights law in Milwaukee since 1970. He had argued cases in both the U.S. District Court for the Eastern District of Wisconsin and its appellate court, the U.S. Court of Appeals for the Seventh Circuit in Chicago, Illinois, as well as the Supreme Court of Wisconsin. First was extremely interested in Joshua's case and agreed to join with Sullivan as cocounsel. He also took over the role of acting as Joshua's guardian ad litem. As it happened, at the time First learned of Joshua's case he was litigating another action that also raised the question of whether the Fourteenth Amendment's protections for personal liberties against state infringement encompassed a state's failure to act. Both cases, *Archie v. City of Racine* and *DeShaney v. Winnebago County Department of Social Services*, followed parallel paths through the courts, beginning in the U.S. District Court for the Eastern District of Wisconsin in Milwaukee and moving to the U.S. Court of Appeals for the Seventh Circuit in Chicago.

The *Archie* case grew out of an incident that occurred in Racine, Wisconsin, in May 1984, just two months after Joshua's final beating. Early one morning a man named Les Hiles called the city fire department because his friend, Rena DeLacy, was having difficulty breathing. After speaking with DeLacy briefly, the dispatcher, George Giese, told her to breathe into a paper bag. Hiles called again that afternoon because DeLacy was still experiencing respiratory problems, and breathing into the paper bag, as the dispatcher suggested, did not help her. Nevertheless, Giese told Hiles that "she's just going to have to breathe into that bag." When questioned, the dispatcher later admitted that he knew Hiles and believed him to be a trouble-maker and a "jerk." DeLacy died that evening of respiratory failure. In the lawsuit Curry First was preparing, DeLacy's estate and her children were suing George Giese, the City of Racine, and the fire chief under the provisions of 42 U.S.C. 1983. The plaintiffs argued that the dispatcher's failure to send the paramedics to help DeLacy violated her rights under the due process clause of the Fourteenth Amendment.

The *Archie* case presented a claim for a citizen's right to enjoy effective rescue services using a doctrine well established in tort law that, although no one is required to rescue another person in distress, if someone begins a rescue he must not be negligent in carrying it out. The general rule that a volunteer rescuer must act competently stems from the notion that the rescuer's attempt may lead other, more able rescuers not to participate, thus leaving the victim worse off than if the rescuer did not begin the attempt. In *Archie*, the plaintiffs were asking the court to apply this doctrine to public services such as the Racine fire department's rescue service. The federal case rested on whether the court accepted the argument that access to city emergency rescue services represented a constitutional right. The question before the court was whether, in establishing emergency rescue services, the state acquired an affirmative duty to carry out a particular rescue. There were, then, important legal similarities between this case and *DeShaney v. Winnebago County*. When Curry First got the call from Sullivan about Joshua's lawsuit, he later recalled, he thought it had the potential to be a "very important case with some cutting edge issues." The suit raised a number of critical questions that at the time were being addressed in the circuit and appellate courts. He knew "within five minutes" of talking with Sullivan over the telephone that he was very interested in joining as cocounsel. After receiving approval from his firm (his work on the case would require considerable time away from his duties there), First accepted Sullivan's offer.

A number of appellate court opinions rendered within the previous six years provided Sullivan and First with a legal path for Joshua's case. Two cases from the Second Circuit were known as *Doe I* (1980) and *Doe II* (1983), both arising from the horrific case of a girl, "Anna Doe," who was physically and sexually abused by her foster father. *Doe I* involved the girl's Section 1983 claim that the agency that had placed her in the home had violated her First, Fourth, Fifth, Ninth, and Fourteenth Amendment rights. (Anna's biological parents and her younger brother were also plaintiffs in the case.) A jury in the district court had found the agency not to be liable. Anna Doe appealed on the grounds that the district court had admitted only portions of the evidence they submitted, leaving out information they believed to be crucial for making their case. Also, Anna claimed that the court's instructions to the jury regarding the defendant's liability had been erroneous because the jury was told that it could only hold the agency liable if it found that it had intended to harm Anna or if it had actual knowledge of the abuse. The appellate court agreed with Anna, deciding that important questions of fact for the jury to decide had indeed been omitted from the trial, and that the district judge's instructions to the jury had ignored relevant precedents indicating additional circumstances in which the agency could be held liable. The court reversed the decision and remanded the case for a new trial. The second jury found in favor of Anna and assessed damages of $225,000, but the trial judge set aside the verdict, saying that the evidence was so overwhelming that "no reasonable jury could have concluded the Bureau acted with deliberate indifference." In *Doe II*, Anna again appealed to the Second Circuit

Court, this time arguing that the *Doe I* decision on appeal meant that the trial court did not have the power to set aside the jury's verdict. The appellate court again decided in favor of Anna, remanding the case for reinstatement of the jury's verdict.

The case law regarding children's claims for a right to bodily security against infringement from state actors was still evolving. A Third Circuit opinion from earlier in 1985 also had potential to help Joshua's case. *Estate of Bailey v. County of York* involved a five-year-old girl named Aleta Bailey who lived with her mother and the mother's boyfriend in York County, Pennsylvania. In January 1982, the child's relatives noticed signs of child abuse on Aleta's body, including severe bruising. When, one week later, the relatives noticed additional bruising, they called the local child abuse prevention hotline as well as the police. The next day, a social worker with the York County Children and Youth Services (YCCYS) took Aleta to the hospital for an examination. The physician advised the social worker that the mother's boyfriend's punishment of the girl was excessive and that he should not have access to the child. Aleta was released from the hospital into the care of her aunt. The YCCYS worker then told the mother that, in order for her to regain custody of Aleta, her boyfriend must move out of her home within twenty-four hours and that she must make arrangements to deny him further access to the girl. Aleta was returned to her mother the following evening despite the fact that the YCCYS did not confirm independently that the conditions for her return had been met; in fact, the three continued to live in the same household. The little girl died one month later from injuries inflicted by both her mother and the mother's boyfriend.

Aleta's father, along with the executor of her estate, sued York County, YCCYS, and the agency's administrator. They charged that the defendants' failure to remove the child from her mother's home violated a Pennsylvania statute that had empowered them to do so if necessary for the child's protection. Further, they argued that YCCYS policies and procedures, based on the family preservation model that privileged keeping a family together, amounted to an abuse of state power, violating the constitutional rights of both Aleta and her father. Aleta had been denied her right to life, the plaintiffs asserted, and the state had taken from her father his constitutional right to parenthood. Although historically legal traditions firmly supported the rights of custodial parents over their children, *Estate of Bailey* asked the court to recognize that children, too, have rights under the U.S. Constitution.

The defendants filed motions to dismiss the case because the plaintiffs had "failed to state a claim upon which relief could be granted," and because they were immune from liability. The motions were granted by the district court, which determined that a state and its agencies were liable for Section 1983 violations under only two circumstances: if a person is injured while in the legal custody of the state, or if the person whose conduct causes the harm is under the control of the state. Aleta, her mother, and the mother's boyfriend were not in the state's custody or control at the time the child was murdered. The appeals court, however, vacated the lower court's dismissal of the suit and sent it on for further proceedings. Judge Sloviter's opinion considered a number of recent circuit court decisions and determined that there was no such "bright line" standard as the lower court had drawn for determining the state's liability. Rather, the precedents suggested that the courts were willing to make much finer distinctions based on the particular facts and circumstances of individual cases. In 1982, for example, the court in *Bowers v. DeVito* had dramatically declared that "if the state puts a man in a position of danger from private persons and then fails to protect him, it will not be heard to say that its role was merely passive; it is as much an active tortfeasor as if it had thrown him into a snake pit."

Two years later, in *Jensen v. Conrad*, the U.S. Court of Appeals for the Fourth Circuit had dismissed a Section 1983 claim against a state and its county social service agencies after a four-month-old girl was killed by her mother's abuse. (An autopsy revealed repeated brain hemorrhages that, before pleading guilty to involuntary manslaughter, the mother initially insisted resulted from the baby "falling out of bed.") But, in dismissing the suit, the court had also rejected the defendants' argument that there existed no right to protection in the absence of a custodial relationship. The requisite "special relationship" may exist under certain circumstances, the court maintained; for instance, if "the state had expressly stated its desire to provide affirmative protection to a particular class of specific individuals," or if the state knew of the victim's plight. Drawing on these recent precedents, the *Bailey* court asserted that there was no reason to assume that Aleta's father and her executor, given the opportunity, would be unable to prove to a jury that the requisite "causal nexus" to establish a special relationship existed between the state's conduct and the death of the girl, and therefore the state was liable. To make Joshua's case, then, Sullivan and First would have to effectively exploit the suggestions apparent in this evolving body of case law.

Sullivan set about gathering the extensive evidence he needed to support the detailed arguments he planned to make before the court. An important element in proving the existence of a special relationship was to demonstrate the degree of contact the Winnebago County DSS had with the DeShaneys over the period of fourteen months during which Joshua was being beaten; the injuries the child received on March 8, 1984, did not represent a single incident of abuse. Sullivan took thorough depositions from a large number of witnesses. The various witnesses were asked questions in order to ascertain, among other things, precisely when Kemmeter and others had witnessed Joshua's various injuries, whether Kemmeter and others were aware that Joshua was being abused in his home, whether her failure to remove him was a violation of generally accepted standards of social work practice, and the extent and permanence of the injuries to Joshua resulting from this failure. Because of the number of witnesses involved as well as the fact that Sullivan lived in Cheyenne and had to travel to Wisconsin where most of the deponents lived, the process stretched over a period of six months, beginning in August 1985 and ending in January 1986. Ultimately, the witness testimony filed in the case totaled no less than 3,742 pages.

Because Sullivan and First originally believed the case would go before a jury in the district court, they also prepared their trial strategy, including questions for selecting the jury during the voir dire process, the witnesses they would call, and an extensive list of exhibits they planned to introduce, including videotapes and photographs of Joshua before and after his final beating, pages from Kemmeter's case notes, charts outlining Joshua's medical expenses, emergency room records and reports, x-rays and CAT scans taken the night of Joshua's emergency neurosurgery, officers' reports from the Neenah and Oshkosh police departments, and models and diagrams of the human brain. Their plans were explicated in the pretrial report the attorneys filed in January 1986. John W. Reynolds, chief judge of the U.S. District Court for the Eastern District of Wisconsin, set a trial date for

{ *Chapter 4* }

the following September. Judge Reynolds was an eminent presence on the bench. A Wisconsin native, World War II veteran, and 1949 graduate of the University of Wisconsin Law School, he served two terms as the state's attorney general before being elected its governor in 1962. Reynolds lost his bid for reelection but was appointed to the federal judiciary by President John F. Kennedy.

Meanwhile, counsel for the defendants diligently prepared their case as well. The two attorneys, Mark Mingo and Wayne Yankala, had been contemporaries at Marquette University Law School in Milwaukee less than ten years earlier and were now with the firm Simarski and Stack in that city. The young attorneys, who had trial and appellate experience, specialized in, among other things, representing both plaintiff and defense parties in medical malpractice suits; they were, therefore, able advocates for the defendants. Curry First later recalled the team as "young hotshots" who "worked very hard and did a very good job" on the case. There was some initial wrangling when Sullivan and First filed a motion alleging possible conflict of interest because one legal team was representing both a public defendant (Winnebago County DSS) and two of the private defendants (Ann Kemmeter and Cheryl Stelse). In the end, however, Mingo and Yankala represented both the public and private parties, and Wisconsin Assistant Attorney General Arnold J. Wightman represented the State of Wisconsin, the Wisconsin Department of Health and Social Services, and its director, Linda Reivetz.

During the extensive discovery process, Mingo and Yankala learned that Mercy Medical Center emergency room physician T. L. Bowers had suspected child abuse when he had examined Joshua and stitched a laceration to his forehead on November 30, 1983. Bowers had delegated the task of completing the official report to a nurse rather than doing it himself. They also learned Oshkosh police officer Paul Michler had indicated his suspicions that Joshua was being harmed in a report he filed after being called to the DeShaney home to investigate a fight between Randy and Marie. Maintaining that their clients Winnebago County DSS did not receive crucial information from either Bowers or the Oshkosh police department pertaining to Joshua's dangerous situation, in September 1985, Mingo and Yankala filed a motion to implead them as third-party defendants. Judge Reynolds did not rule on the motion (the reason for which is not clear from the public record).

The following month, Mingo and Yankala submitted a motion to dismiss the case against their clients on three grounds. First, the attorneys argued, Melody and Joshua did not have a viable claim because the Fourteenth Amendment "does not include a constitutionally protected right to child protective services." Under the Federal Rules for Civil Procedure, the plaintiffs had failed "to state a claim upon which relief can be granted" and therefore the case must be dismissed from federal court. Secondly, defendants Ann Kemmeter and Cheryl Stelse enjoyed immunity from the suit. Recent court rulings, they argued, had found that government officials could not be held liable for an alleged wrong if the law was not clearly established at the time it occurred. In the 1980s, there was no clearly established body of federal law governing the duties of state child protective services toward their clients. Thirdly, Mingo and Yankala asserted that there was not a sufficient "causal nexus" between the defendants and the injuries Joshua had received at the hands of his father. Here the defendants relied on a 1980 U.S. Supreme Court ruling, *Martinez v. California*, for support. In that case, a convicted sex offender released on parole five months earlier murdered a fifteen-year-old girl. The girl's surviving relatives sued the state officials responsible for making the decision to parole the offender. California law provided immunity for the officials, so the plaintiffs brought their case to federal court under Section 1983, charging that the officials' actions amounted to the state depriving the girl of her right to life under the Fourteenth Amendment. Writing for the majority, Justice John Paul Stevens upheld a lower court's opinion that the girl's death was "too remote a consequence of the parole board's action to hold them responsible under the federal civil rights law." The state employees were not liable simply because their actions had set off a chain of events that ultimately led to the death of the girl. Mingo and Yankala argued that any actions taken by their defendants were likewise remote in the chain of events that had led to Joshua's final beating by his father. They stressed that the purely voluntary nature of the social service agreement between the Winnebago County DSS and Randy DeShaney necessarily reduced to zero the degree of control, and therefore responsibility, the state agents had in the incident.

In January 1986, Judge Reynolds informed the parties of his intent to convert the defendants' motion for dismissal into a motion for "summary judgment." A summary judgment allows the court to render a swift decision rather than sending the case on to a full jury trial. The procedure is most commonly used in civil lawsuits. A summary judgment may be made in regard to one or more undisputed issues of fact in the case (thereby reducing the number of facts given to a jury to decide) or, if enough of the facts are undisputed, the summary judgment is rendered as a matter of law. The defendants in a lawsuit usually file the motion. They must convince the court that their opponents have raised no genuine issue of fact or of law to be brought before a jury. In considering the motion, the court is obligated to regard all materials in a light that is most favorable to the plaintiffs. Under Rule 56 of the Federal Rules of Civil Procedure, "the court must treat a motion for judgment on the pleadings or a motion to dismiss for failure to state a claim upon which relief may be granted as a motion for summary judgment if matters outside the pleadings are presented to the court." Judge Reynolds determined that *both* of the parties had introduced matters outside of the pleadings, thereby triggering Rule 56.

The summary judgment procedure also allows the court to consider a wide variety of "outside" materials before granting the motion. Accordingly, Judge Reynolds gave the parties thirty days to submit any additional briefs, affidavits, and depositions garnered from their extensive preparations. He also ordered both the Neenah and Oshkosh police departments to make their files on the DeShaney family available to the court (where they became part of the public record). Later that month Judge Reynolds dismissed the suit against the State of Wisconsin and the Wisconsin Department of Health and Social Services, citing the Eleventh Amendment's provision that states enjoy sovereign immunity in federal courts unless they consent to be sued there. Since the plaintiffs had made no allegations concerning the personal involvement of Linda Reivetz in Joshua's case, he dismissed the suit against her as well.

The possibility of a summary judgment presented a serious strategic problem for Sullivan and First. They had been counting on presenting their voluminous evidence to a jury in support of their argument that a "special relationship" existed between the Winnebago County DSS and Joshua DeShaney. The two attorneys were especially alarmed that Judge Reynolds's decision to convert the defendants' motion to dismiss into a motion for summary judgment intimated that no factual issues were being disputed between the parties. Sullivan and First believed that, on the contrary, their argument supporting the special relationship claim — in opposition to the defendants' argument that no such relationship had existed — required the court to consider *all* of the extensive factual evidence they had planned to offer. To a significant degree, their argument depended on the *quantity* of the evidence in the case. They filed a brief opposing the motion for summary judgment as well as two separate motions of their own asking permission to file the full transcripts of several depositions (as opposed to only excerpts cited in their brief) for the court's review. The court's permission was needed because a local rule prohibited the filing of complete depositions without leave of the court. Judge Reynolds, however, did not rule on their requests. (Again, there is no clear explanation in the public record for his failure to do so.)

For their part, the defendants filed an additional brief charging that the plaintiffs "have desperately attempted to create a vague and nebulous special relationship between the County defendants and Joshua DeShaney." Although admitting that the lower courts had at times taken an inconsistent approach, Mingo and Yankala argued that *very* recent court rulings — decisions, in fact, handed down within the previous forty-five days — clearly demonstrated that the courts did not want to "allow 42 U.S.C. Section 1983 to be manipulated and extended beyond its original scope and purpose." The rulings came from two U.S. Supreme Court cases, *Daniels v. Williams* and *Davidson v. Cannon.* Justice William H. Rehnquist had written both opinions. The *Daniels* case involved a prison inmate who had sustained injuries by slipping on a pillow negligently left on some stairs. He filed a Section 1983 suit against prison officials claiming a violation of his Fourteenth Amendment rights. He also invoked a "special relationship" in order to convert a common law tort into a federal civil rights action. The nation's High Court dismissed the prisoner's case, noting that "the guarantee of due process is a guarantee against arbitrary action of the government used for purposes of oppression." The pillow incident did not rise to this level of due process protection; the Supreme Court "refused to 'trivialize' the century-old principle of due process of law." Mingo and Yankala further noted that Justice Rehnquist had invoked the great Chief Justice John Marshall's 1819 admonition that "we must never forget that it is a *constitution* we are expounding," with the inference that personal injury cases do not normally rise to the level of a constitutional challenge. Therefore, the attorneys argued, because Joshua's case likewise sought to convert a common law tort into a Section 1983 claim, it should be dismissed as well.

The other U.S. Supreme Court opinion to which Mingo and Yankala referred arose from a case involving an inmate who had tried to warn prison officials that he was in danger after he had received threats from other inmates; he later was assaulted. Davidson claimed that, in failing to prevent the assault, the officials had violated his constitutional rights. Davidson's Section 1983 claim was also dismissed by the nation's High Court because, although the officials' negligence had resulted in serious injury, such a lack of care "simply does not approach the sort of abusive government conduct that the due process clause was designed to prevent." The attorneys quoted Justice Rehnquist's assertion that "the guarantee of due process has never been understood to mean that the State must guarantee due care on the part of its officials." Mingo and Yankala argued that, if the Supreme Court had determined that no special relationship existed under the facts of these recent cases, then "clearly, the plaintiff's contention in the instant case that there exists a 'special relationship' between county defendants and the DeShaney family must fall." The brief did not address the question of whether these rulings were pertinent to Joshua's situation given that he was a four-year-old child being brutalized in his home while the state failed to administer "due care."

A third recent decision referenced in the defendants' brief was *Archie v. City of Racine*, Curry First's other case in the district court, which had been decided the previous February by Judge Terence T. Evans. Evans had also rejected the special relationship argument, concluding that "there is nothing in the constitution which requires governmental units to act when members of the general public are in danger." Similarly, Mingo and Yankala contended, the state's offer of voluntary family services through the Winnebago County DSS did not create a special relationship giving rise to an affirmative duty to protect the children of Wisconsin. To hold that it did, they continued, "would be to expose each and every similar department to such liability each and every time it chose to extend voluntary services to a family." States would actually limit protections for children if they feared being sued when the protections failed. Taken together, the attorneys asserted, these very recent rulings made it clear that Joshua's claim would not stand up in court at this time. A summary judgment in the case was therefore entirely appropriate.

On June 20, 1986, Reynolds granted the motion for summary judgment requested by Winnebago County DSS, Kemmeter, and Stelse. His decision began with a succinct summary of the facts of the case. In this construction of Joshua's story, the boy's physical injuries were observed by several people. Notably absent, however, are any references to Kemmeter's case notes in which she had mused about the possibility that his injuries were being caused by the abusive adults in his home. Reynolds's narrative, therefore, presents the story as though a number of warning signs of physical abuse were merely missed by the child protective worker. In this version, Kemmeter had simply failed to pay sufficient attention to her clients. Accordingly, the decision concludes that the plaintiff's claims are "sound in state tort law." Thus, Reynolds left the door open for a future civil lawsuit in state court where the facts — as they were now constructed — might meet the lower threshold for establishing that the state agents had been negligent. (This would be the kind of "garden variety" lawsuit Sullivan had been sure that Joshua would win, but the low cap Wisconsin set on damages he could recover would be nearly worthless in providing for the boy's actual needs.)

But Melody and Joshua could make no claims in federal court according to Reynolds, who noted that, under *Jackson v. City of Joliet*, citizens do not have a right to basic public services. "The Constitution is a charter of negative liberties," the court had maintained in 1983; "it tells the state to let people alone; it does not require the federal government or the state to provide services." But, the judge continued, "if a government places an individual in a position of danger from private persons, it creates or assumes a special relationship," from which a duty to provide protective services may arise. (Here Reynolds quoted the "snake pit" metaphor from *Bowers v. DeVito*.) He noted examples in which previous courts had established an affirmative duty to protect, including *White v. Rochford* and *Spence v. Staras*. However, he determined that Joshua's case was not "sufficiently similar" to these cases to support the claim that a special relationship existed. Judge Reynolds next addressed the question of whether the criteria for state liability established in *Estate of Bailey* could be applied to Joshua's case. They could not, he decided, for two reasons. First, Reynolds determined that the U.S. Supreme Court's very recent rulings in *Davidson* and *Daniels* had reinforced a more rigid standard as the proper basis for granting a Section 1983 claim. Such a claim, according to the Supreme Court, must establish "arbitrary use of governmental power for purposes of oppression." Second, he rejected as "unsound" the *Bailey* court's position that one criterion for holding a state liable might be the state's desire to affirmatively protect a particular class or specific individuals. If this standard were to be adopted, Reynolds warned, "every social welfare program would thus become a charter of constitutionally sanctioned social and economic 'rights' which . . . require much more than the restraint of power to guarantee." Given these determinations, then, the court agreed with the defendants that no real issues of law remained to be decided and he granted their motion for summary judgment. The case would not proceed to a full jury trial.

Curry First later recalled his extreme disappointment, as well as his unhappy surprise, at Reynolds's decision. He believed that, through the evolving case law, there was enough support in the lower courts for the legal theories he and Sullivan had presented in their brief for the court to allow the case to go forward to a full trial. On a personal level, he liked and respected Reynolds. But First was also Joshua's guardian ad litem, and he knew that his premier duty was to act in the best interests of the boy. He had envisioned one scenario in which Joshua would win his case in the district court and then, rather than letting the case be appealed, his counsel would settle with Winnebago County for a dollar amount sufficient to meet Joshua's extremely expensive medical needs. As it now stood, the boy remained in the custody of Winnebago County and was receiving care at the public's expense. Additional funds, however, would enable Joshua to be treated by higher quality, possibly private, medical professionals and services with potentially better results for the child. Given the loss in the district court, then, First felt strongly that the case should be appealed to give Joshua his chance for superior care. But he was worried about their chances of winning in the U.S. Court of Appeals for the Seventh Circuit, which did not have a record of supporting claims for the expansion of civil rights. And, he recalled, he distinctly did not want the case to go before the nation's High Court, which had very recently issued two opinions (*Davidson* and *Daniels*) that boded ill for Joshua's chances there. First recalled feeling that he did not want to give the Supreme Court the opportunity to "make bad law."

Donald Sullivan also recalled his extreme disappointment. He had visited Joshua in the foster home and had seen the child's rigid posture, the very limited and awkward use of his limbs, and his use of sounds rather than language. Although Joshua had not remained at the Gillette Center in St. Paul (it is unclear from the public record whether the move was due to financial or other considerations), he had been receiving physical and occupational therapy in his foster homes in Wisconsin. Sullivan recalled watching Joshua, propped on pillows so that he could sit upright, practicing the grip in his right hand by attempting to pick up Cheerios. The boy could turn his head and eyes toward voices in the room, and he could make vocalizations expressing happiness. The attorney recalled thinking "this is a kid, and this is a hurt kid." He thought it was "an easy call" to appeal Joshua's case since the only other option was to "just give up" — a choice Sullivan found unacceptable. And he was less apprehensive than his cocounsel was about Joshua's chances in the legal system. In fact, Sullivan had always "strongly suspected that we were going to get to the Supreme Court." And, he believed, Joshua would win.

CHAPTER 5

DeShaney v. Winnebago County in the U.S. Supreme Court

On July 23, 1986, just over a month following the district court's decision to grant the motion by the defendants (now consisting of the Winnebago County DSS, Ann Kemmeter, and Cheryl Stelse) for summary judgment, Sullivan and First learned that Joshua's case would go before the U.S. Court of Appeals for the Seventh Circuit in Chicago, Illinois. But the turnaround time the court had scheduled was very short, prompting the attorneys to file a motion asking the court to extend the deadline for filing their briefs. Despite objections from Winnebago County, the extension was granted, and Sullivan and First now faced a deadline of September 12, 1986, for submitting their appeal. After some minor procedural snafus (Sullivan had used the wrong color covers on the appellants' brief and it had to be resubmitted), the briefs were filed in due order and oral arguments set for January 13, 1987. The three-judge panel hearing the case consisted of Richard A. Posner and John L. Coffey, circuit judges, and Robert A. Grant, district judge for the Northern District of Indiana (sitting by designation). Interestingly, both sides in the case filed petitions for the arguments to be heard *en banc*, or before the entire court, but their motions were denied.

The brief Sullivan and First filed on behalf of Joshua framed six questions for the court's review. The first asked whether the "refusal of a social worker to protect a child from a known high risk of severe child abuse, given repeated indicia of severe ongoing abuse brought to the workers' attention over a period of fourteen months" was actionable under Section 1983 (the section of the U.S. Code that allows citizens to bring civil lawsuits to federal court claiming there has been a violation of their constitutional rights). Next, Sullivan and First set out a series of questions that asked the court to confirm that the requisite "special relationship" existed that gave rise to an affirmative duty on the part of the Winnebago County DSS to protect Joshua (see Chapter Four), whether its failure to act constituted "reckless indifference" or "gross negligence," and whether the absence of a legal relationship between Randy DeShaney and the DSS absolved the agency of liability when "there was actual reason to believe the abuse was occurring and [there was] actual opportunity over a long period of time to intervene to protect the child." Essentially, Joshua's lawyers asked the appeals court to consider their argument that the Fourteenth Amendment's due process protections for life and liberty extended to Joshua's right to be protected from his father's violence and, if he had such a right, to hold Wisconsin's child protection services liable for its failure to safeguard it.

The brief then turned from the actions of the Wisconsin DSS to the actions of the circuit court in Milwaukee. Sullivan and First alleged that the lower court's actions had been anomalous in terms of legal procedure. Judge Reynolds had converted Winnebago County's reply brief into a Rule 56 motion for summary judgment because he found that factual matters existed outside of both parties' complaints. He then ordered both sides to submit additional briefs, affidavits, and depositions. Sullivan and First, however, had filed an objection to the motion for summary judgment as well as two additional motions asking permission to file the full transcripts of several depositions (in accordance with a local rule), believing that the court needed to see the extensive nature of their evidence in order to find that a "special relationship" did in fact exist between Joshua and the DSS. But, the attorneys asserted, Reynolds made no ruling at all on their motions and, as a consequence, the court had failed to consider the "extensive factual proofs" they had intended to offer. Instead, the court dismissed Joshua's case because it was not sufficiently similar to cases in which other courts had found a special relationship existed between state agents and citizens. Yet the court had not considered evidence that the attorneys believed would have demonstrated that very similarity. For example, the court in *Spence v. Staras* had found a special relationship between prison guards and inmates, holding them liable when guards had knowingly exposed an inmate to the risk of assault. The attorneys wanted to argue that Joshua, although technically not an "inmate," nevertheless had been thoroughly enmeshed in a child welfare system in which *only* the Winnebago County DSS could have protected him. But without examining the briefs that would have detailed the extensive nature of DSS's involvement with the DeShaneys, the lower court had refused to find the special relationship required to confirm an affirmative duty to protect Joshua. Having made this charge, the attorneys concluded with an extensive summation detailing the agency's fourteen-month relationship with the DeShaneys.

Attorneys for DSS countered that the allegedly negligent conduct of Ann Kemmeter and the Winnebago County DSS was irrelevant because Joshua's essential claim that their actions constituted a deprivation of his constitutionally protected right had no merit in itself. Simply put, if no such constitutional right existed, then there could be no deprivation of the right, regardless of the state's actions (or nonactions). Mark Mingo and Wayne Yankala argued that the "special relationship" criteria that would invoke the state's liability must be strictly construed, limited to those cases in which state actors engaged in some affirmative act that actually placed an individual in harm's way. Although the DSS had taken custody of Joshua briefly during his first hospital stay in early 1983, the child protective team had determined that no child abuse had occurred and, upon returning Joshua to his father's custody, the agency had closed his official case file. All subsequent contact, they asserted, had been in the form of a strictly voluntary agreement between Randy DeShaney and the DSS that, unlike a court-ordered treatment plan, Randy was free to break at any time. Under such circumstances, Kemmeter and the DSS could not be held liable for the subsequent abuse Joshua endured in his father's home.

The appellate court issued its opinion on February 12, 1987, one month after it heard oral arguments in the case. Judge Posner, a prolific legal scholar who had clerked for U.S. Supreme Court Justice William J. Brennan from 1962 to 1963, began by stating the facts "as favorably to the plaintiffs as the record will allow," in keeping with the rules for summary judgment. He then put forward two possible theories by which the defendants might have violated Joshua's rights to a form of liberty or property under the Fourteenth Amendment's due process clause. The first theory — that the DSS had deprived Joshua of a constitutional right to be protected from his father's violence — Posner dismissed by "the rule, well established in this circuit," that a state's failure to protect a citizen from violence inflicted by a private actor does not deprive the citizen of a constitutional right." Posner referred to "the principle that the Constitution is a charter of negative rather than positive liberties." Although he acknowledged the existence of some exceptions to this principle (for example, a state denying its protection to a disfavored minority could be said to be in violation of the Fourteenth Amendment's equal protection clause), the judge found none of these exceptions applicable to Joshua's case. "The state does not have a duty enforceable by the federal courts," he continued, "to maintain a police force or a fire department, or to protect children from their parents. The men who framed the original Constitution and the Fourteenth Amendment were worried about government's oppressing the citizenry rather than about its failing to provide adequate social services." Failures of a state agency such as those perpetrated by the Winnebago County DSS were, for the judge, subject to remedy through state courts or legislatures.

The second theory Posner considered was that the state had been complicit in the beatings that had left Joshua "essentially immobilized for life," creating a deprivation of the boy's liberty under the due process clause. "The question," he wrote, "is whether the state shares responsibility for this deprivation, in a federal constitutional sense, with Joshua's father." Like Reynolds in the lower court, Posner found the Winnebago County DSS "blameworthy" in the poor performance of its state-designated role. However, he also found that it "did not appreciably increase the probability of Joshua's injuries" in doing so. For Posner, the question to ask was whether Joshua would have sustained the injuries if the DSS had never existed. The answer, he determined was yes. "It is unlikely that Ann Kemmeter's well-intentioned but ineffectual intervention did Joshua any good at all, but is most unlikely that it did him any harm. She merely failed to protect him from his bestial father." Posner then addressed the question of whether Joshua's case fit the "botched rescue attempt" model in common tort law (see Chapter Four). He, like Reynolds in the lower court, determined that the liability here was a question to be determined by the state rather than the federal courts. "A state can if it wants," he wrote, "whether acting through its courts or its legislature, impose tort duties on persons who fail to rescue someone whose peril they did not cause — whose liberty they did not take away — but a constitutional tort requires deprivation by the defendant, and not merely a failure to protect the plaintiff from a danger created by others." Thus, Posner rejected the second theory by which the Winnebago County DSS could be said to have deprived Joshua of his constitutional rights.

Finally, the court addressed the crucial question of whether a "special relationship" existed between DSS and the DeShaneys. The three-judge panel rejected the Third Circuit's determination in *Estate of Bailey* (see Chapter Four) that a special relationship — resulting in a constitutional duty to protect — occurs once a state becomes aware that a particular child may be undergoing abuse in his home. "We can find no basis in the language of the due process clauses or the principles of constitutional law for a general doctrine of 'special relationship,'" Posner asserted. Further, the court believed that extending the special relationship theory to Joshua's case "would inject the federal courts into an area in which they have little knowledge or experience: child welfare," an area best left to state regulation and oversight. He envisioned a scenario in which state social welfare agencies throughout the nation would be forced to walk a "razor's edge," vulnerable to federal lawsuits if they acted too aggressively in removing children from their parents' homes but equally vulnerable if they failed to take action to protect children from their parents' violence.

Sullivan and First were not especially surprised with the appeals court's ruling, given that Posner's view that the Constitution was a "charter of negative liberties" was well known through his many legal writings. (Sullivan did, however, later admit to feeling extremely unlucky that the case had drawn Judge Posner in the Seventh Circuit's rotation.) Less than two weeks later, the attorneys petitioned the Seventh Circuit for a rehearing of the case *en banc*, or before the full court. Sullivan later recalled feeling frustrated by his belief that Posner's opinion had misstated their case in assuming that finding in favor of Joshua meant placing social service agencies on the "razor's edge," constantly exposed to the possibility of federal lawsuits. For Sullivan, the court simply ducked its obligation to draw the line itself between parental rights and state responsibility for ensuring children's safety in their parents' homes. He viewed Kemmeter's actions in the fourteen months preceding Joshua's final beating as so egregious that they had afforded the court the opportunity to set a minimum standard for protecting children. "Maybe you get ten free passes," he later said, "but at some point you are responsible." Among the arguments Sullivan and

First made in their brief was the one that the U.S. Supreme Court had, in *Daniels v. Williams* and *Davidson v. Cannon* (see Chapter Four) noted that, although those two cases considered ordinary negligence, the Court awaited a future case in which to take up the questions of misconduct going beyond simple negligence — and Sullivan believed Joshua's tragic story clearly represented that case. In fact, the attorney charged that Posner's opinion had significantly misstated the factual setting of the case because it focused on Joshua's final beating only — an event that the court determined had been unforeseeable by Kemmeter. But framing the facts this way, Sullivan argued, ignored the details alleged in Joshua's complaint that the child was being *systematically* brutalized over a period of fourteen months during which "the child protection workers not only had reason to know it but in fact did know it and believe it, and admitted as much." Sullivan characterized DSS's failure to act to protect Joshua as "a shrugging of the shoulders, a yawning at another's peril" that, having occurred over an extended period of time, amounted to something much more offensive than a "mere single act of 'whoops.'" Given these reprehensible facts, Sullivan dramatically asserted, Posner's ruling implied that "a public entity has no liability whatever, except in the single circumstance where the public employee physically wields the club that shatters the flesh and bone." Therefore, he concluded, a rehearing of the case before the full Seventh Circuit court was appropriate. On April 21, 1987, however, the petition was denied.

Three months later, Joshua's case was appealed to the U.S. Supreme Court, and on March 21, 1988, the Court agreed to hear it. Joshua's petition for a writ of certiorari — the official procedure requesting a hearing in the nation's High Court — was granted when Justices Byron White, Harry Blackmun, William Brennan, and Thurgood Marshall voted to hear the case. The Court was keenly aware of the potential pitfalls of wading into an area of civil rights law still in an early — and much contested — stage of development in the lower courts. The "cert pool" — law clerks charged with reviewing writs of certiorari and making recommendations about their acceptance to the justices — counseled caution, urging that "despite the special facts of this case it might be appropriate to defer consideration of the issue until there is a more well-defined circuit split." Even Justice Blackmun, who voted to hear the case, noted to his clerk Edward B. Foley that "this is a dangerous area and must be carefully delineated." In the end, it was Justice White's vote that brought the vote for acceptance to the requisite number of four. Justice White, apparently, saw no clear purpose in delaying consideration of the issue. (He later voted against Joshua in the Court's ruling in the case.)

At this point, a new party entered the picture, the Children's Rights Project of the American Civil Liberties Union (ACLU). For more than ten years, the Children's Rights Project had been working to carve out what was essentially new terrain in civil rights law. Drawing from the ACLU's two decades of work involving adult prisoners' cases, the project had brought a number of successful federal class action suits on behalf of children in foster care systems throughout the United States. Christopher A. Hansen of the ACLU later recalled becoming aware of the case when it was filed in the Seventh Circuit and contacting Sullivan. In March 1987, Hansen and his colleague on the project, Marcia Robinson Lowry, had submitted an amicus curiae (friend of the court) brief in support of Joshua's petition for a rehearing of his case before the full court. The project's lawyers had argued that Posner's ruling left "hundreds of thousands of children in jeopardy of slipshod and negligent practices by agencies established and funded to protect them from the foreseeable brutality to which Joshua DeShaney was subjected." They faulted Posner's reasoning, which equated Joshua with any other child in the general population under the legal custodianship of his father. Rather, they argued, Joshua was a child "whom the county already knew to be entitled to the protections of a federally funded county child welfare agency." The state, they continued, had created the child protection system and, in so doing, had accepted responsibility for Joshua under both Wisconsin and federal law governing child welfare provision. Because the DSS had acted "in a way it knew would result in harm" to Joshua, it had effectively denied him the intended benefits of the state and federal laws, "that of reasonable protection from an abusive parent." Federal statutes, they continued, conditioned state child welfare systems' receipt of federal funding on providing adequate services, including taking immediate steps to protect an abused child "as well as any other child under the same care who may be in danger of abuse or neglect."

Contrary to the panel's opinion that the federal government had no expertise in child welfare, such issues had already been taken on by the federal courts.

Lawyers with the Children's Rights Project believed a crucial foundational precedent to be the U.S. Supreme Court's 1982 ruling in *Youngberg v. Romeo*, a case involving a severely mentally impaired adult male who had received numerous physical injuries — caused by himself and others — while living in a state institution in Pennsylvania. Romeo's mother had brought suit against the institution, charging that the staff's failure to protect her son from injuries violated his rights under the Fourteenth Amendment. Writing for the majority, Justice Lewis F. Powell had affirmed that the amendment does indeed afford individuals a right to personal security. Children's Rights Project lawyers would later argue (in the amicus brief they filed in support of Joshua in the U.S. Supreme Court) that the "existence of that [personal security] right does not and should not depend on whether Joshua was in the formal legal custody of the state or in the state's institutional care." Rather, they continued, "the critical question is whether . . . the state voluntarily and affirmatively assumed responsibility for the protection of a specific individual when (1) that individual was unable to protect himself and (2) the state's assumption of responsibility effectively precluded others from protecting him" — two criteria that applied, they would argue, as much to four-year-old Joshua DeShaney as to an adult confined to a state mental institution. For the ACLU lawyers, *DeShaney v. Winnebago County* represented an important opportunity to further the goals of the Children's Rights Project.

But the exact nature of the ACLU's role in Joshua's case was also a source of some tension between Sullivan and First. When it became clear that *DeShaney v. Winnebago County* would be going before the U.S. Supreme Court, First later recalled, he had urged his partner in the case to allow the Children's Rights Project to take over. "I realized that Don Sullivan and I," First later recalled, "in terms of experience at the Supreme Court and with this issue, were completely . . . out of our league." First was impressed with the amicus brief that Chris Hansen and others associated with the Children's Rights Project were preparing. "I wanted every quality resource we could get," he remarked. Eventually, several other children's rights advocacy organizations joined the ACLU on the amicus brief, including the

Wisconsin branch of the ACLU, Legal Services for Children, the Juvenile Law Center, the Bay Area Coalition Against Child Abuse, and the National Woman Abuse Prevention Project. First also recalled that he was "constantly talking to Chris" while Joshua's case was being prepared. But Sullivan resisted the idea of the Children's Rights Project taking over at the helm. Sullivan was the only attorney in the case who had met Joshua and Melody and had observed first-hand the devastating consequences of Joshua's plight. Despite the lower court rulings, Sullivan still believed that "if there can ever be liability of a social worker for harm that was inflicted by a third person, if we can have that as a constitutional possibility ever, the facts of this case are so extreme that we [will] win." Ultimately, although the ACLU lawyers made significant contributions to *DeShaney v. Winnebago County*, Sullivan remained as lead counsel in the case.

A significant addition to the prior arguments made on behalf of Joshua in the lower courts appeared in the Supreme Court brief filed on August 12, 1988. The attorneys stated the claim that the provisions of the Wisconsin Children's Code created an entitlement of child protective services for Joshua, and thus the state's denial of them constituted a violation of his due process rights under the Fourteenth Amendment. This claim was drawn from *Board of Regents v. Roth*, a 1972 opinion in which the High Court had stated that, in appropriate circumstances, a state statute may "create a benefit which amounts to an entitlement and enjoys due process protections." The Wisconsin statutes, the plaintiffs' brief asserted, were "clear and specific in their intent affirmatively to recognize and protect children who are endangered by abuse or neglect." Further, the Children's Code set forth mandatory obligations on the part of the Department of Social Services, including the nondiscretionary duty to open a new, formal investigation upon each report of abuse or neglect it receives. The clear statutory role the law prescribed for the state's child protective workers preempted the ability of other possible protectors (doctors, nurses, police officers, relatives, neighbors, etc.) to act on Joshua's behalf. Thus, according to the brief, the DSS "not only promised to protect him but stripped him of the other persons who could, absent this scheme, have intervened on his behalf." The state's enactment of the Children's Code and the explicit — and exclusive — role it had created for state child protective workers in investigating abuse amounted to an entitlement, in the sense outlined in *Board of Regents v. Roth*, for Joshua; Winnebago County DSS's failure to follow its procedural obligations under the law thus resulted in a violation of Joshua's due process rights.

Amid the tensions as the attorneys got ready for their Supreme Court date, another development further complicated their preparations. In June 1988 Sullivan announced his candidacy for a seat in the Wyoming state legislature, entering a crowded field of Democrats in the primary election held in August. The *Wyoming State Tribune* quoted the candidate contrasting himself with the "theory and dry dust in the Legislature. I want to be a human being, caring for other human beings," Sullivan said, adding that in his work as a lawyer he met many people who "are truly down and out, and when tackling issues like economic development he would think of it in terms of 'putting food on the table for families.'" Successfully jumping the primary hurdle, Sullivan began his campaign for the election to be held on November 8, just six days after oral arguments in *DeShaney v. Winnebago County* were scheduled to be heard before the Supreme Court. The time and attention Sullivan devoted to his campaign in Wyoming distressed Melody DeShaney, who was working as a waitress in Phoenix at the time. She was confused about what was happening to Joshua's case and angry that Sullivan was not returning her telephone calls. She also wanted the attorney's office to cover the airfare to Washington, D.C., so that she could attend oral arguments. William Glaberson, a reporter who had interviewed Melody for the *New York Times Magazine*, remembered thinking at the time that she was "distinctly over her head," upset and angry because the publicity given to the case had created the impression she was a bad mother. Her second marriage was in the process of dissolving, and she told Graberson she had few friends to whom she could turn for support in this stressful time. Melody then took the extraordinary step of sending a handwritten note to Chief Justice Rehnquist expressing her dissatisfaction with her representation by Sullivan and First and informing the Court that she wanted new attorneys. First later described this time as "the lowest point in my life as a lawyer." Just four days before Sullivan and First were scheduled to appear before the nation's High Court, the attorneys spoke with Melody via a conference call arranged by Winnebago Circuit Court Judge Thomas S. Williams. Given the opportunity to air her grievances, Melody's anxiety was assuaged and the matter was resolved. For First, this distressing incident just days before he left for Washington, D.C., represented "the most dramatic thing in the case."

Like Sullivan and First, the team of Mingo and Yankala also sought expert help in preparing their Supreme Court case. The attorneys turned to the Washington, D.C., firm of Onek, Klein, and Farr, established in 1981 as a "boutique" firm working exclusively in the area of appellate and Supreme Court litigation. All three attorneys, although young, had already gained extensive experience practicing at the federal level. H. Barton Farr had only a few years earlier clerked for Justice Rehnquist, and Joseph Onek had served as President Jimmy Carter's deputy counsel and clerked for Justice Brennan. Both attorneys also subsequently enjoyed illustrious legal careers in both private practice and public service. The two lawyers who joined Mingo and Yankala on the respondents' brief in *DeShaney v. Winnebago County* were David A. Bono and Joel L. Klein. (After the breakup of Onek, Klein, and Farr, Bono represented federal agencies in numerous court cases and Joel Klein served as deputy counsel to President William Clinton.)

Their brief offered a narrative of the relationship between the DSS and the DeShaney family that stressed the "voluntary" nature of their agreement, noting that the services Kemmeter offered were, according to her notes, delineated under the social service categories of "Individual and Family Adjustment," "Education," "Employment," and "Health." Further, Kemmeter had "focused her efforts on proper parenting and appropriate disciplinary techniques" and observed the family "when circumstances permitted." It is interesting to note that, under this construction, the service categories appear to be somewhat independent of the larger purpose of preventing child abuse using the family preservation model. In the social worker's own notes, the list of services actually had been listed under the stated "goal" of "protection," with the "primary objective" consisting of the "resolution of abuse, neglect, or exploitation" (see Chapter One). Viewed in the full context of the social worker's report, therefore, it seems apparent that the ultimate goal of Kemmeter's involvement with the DeShaneys was to safeguard Joshua rather than to provide the listed services per se. The family preservation model employed social service categories as the *means* for preventing child abuse, not merely as ends in and of themselves. The description provided in the brief, however, elides the two functions.

Nor did the respondents' brief emphasize that, under Wisconsin law, as a "child protective worker," Kemmeter was also assigned the responsibility of observing the family for signs of abuse, whether the DSS agreement with Randy DeShaney was voluntary or not. The brief described Kemmeter as noting her "concern" and "suspicion" about the possibility of domestic violence but stressed that, because Kemmeter had believed that none of it could be "proven" and that none of the injuries were "serious enough to warrant court intervention," no action was taken by DSS. "Prior to March 9, 1984 [the day after Joshua's final beating]," the brief continued, "there were no further reports of suspected child abuse of the kind that would have been sufficient to trigger an investigation" under Wisconsin law.

Interestingly, the attorneys' use of the passive voice here carries an implication that Kemmeter was dependent on others to report possible abuse occurring to Joshua rather than a DSS employee carrying the specific job title of "child protective worker." Further, there is no mention of the fact that Kemmeter did not actually see Joshua for a period of four months prior to his final beating in March 1984, a period in which the Oshkosh police made repeated visits to the DeShaney home responding to reports of physical fighting between Randy and Marie. The brief characterizes as "inaccurate, unsupported, and unfair" a number of accusations by Joshua's attorneys and the ACLU that numerous reports of Joshua's abuse were ignored by DSS because in fact these had been reports of injuries to the child rather than diagnoses of child abuse. The brief does not address the fact that Kemmeter had accepted the explanations she received from Randy and Marie without investigating further to determine whether they were indeed "accidents." The authors give the example that, upon having visited the DeShaneys in November 1983, Kemmeter had merely "wondered" whether marks on Joshua's chin were the result of cigarette burns and, upon questioning the parents, "they stated that Joshua had been outside and had scraped his chin on the sidewalk." Kemmeter's lack of further concern about the incident, therefore, could be readily explained. (Interestingly, the account given in the reply brief is itself inaccurate. According to Kemmeter's own notes, when she had asked Marie about the marks on Joshua's chin, Marie directed the boy to explain what had happened whereupon he knelt down on his hands and knees and rubbed his own face on the sidewalk. Kemmeter detailed this unusual behavior in her notes, but apparently did not find it worthy of further investigation.)

The real violence against Joshua, the brief's argument made clear, was perpetrated by Randy DeShaney, not the Winnebago County DSS. Joshua's fate was tragic but his constitutional rights, protected from infringement by the state under the Fourteenth Amendment's due process clause, had not been violated since "there is no generalized duty on a state or municipality to provide affirmative protection to members of the public at large." The petitioners' efforts to "transform a privately inflicted harm into a governmental deprivation," the brief asserted, "stretches the Due Process Clause well beyond its breaking point." Further, Joshua's attorneys had not proved that Kemmeter and the DSS had acted with the "requisite state of mind" to commit a due process violation. Rejecting the lawyers' labeling of Kemmeter's inaction as "gross negligence or recklessness," the brief asserted that the only remaining standard for determining that the "requisite state of mind" existed was "deliberate indifference" — a standard that the facts of the case failed to satisfy. "It cannot plausibly be claimed," the brief argued, "that Respondents acted with deliberate indifference toward any rights the Petitioner may have had. On the contrary, for more than a year they provided voluntary counseling to the DeShaney family." Although a tragedy had certainly occurred, it was "hardly the product of any purposeful or deliberate indifference" on the part of the social services department.

Further, Kemmeter and the DSS staff had exercised their professional judgment and determined there was insufficient evidence that child abuse was occurring in the DeShaney home. Far from being indifferent to the family, they had "acted with sensitivity to the parental rights at stake here," by not removing the child from his father's custody without "clear and convincing" evidence of abuse — a standard mandated by both Wisconsin law and the U.S. Constitution. Additionally, the standard Joshua's attorneys were proposing would "place increasing pressure on state agencies to *interfere* with individual liberty by removing children from their families out of fear that otherwise the State will be held liable for the resultant harms," a disturbing prospect for family privacy rights. Finally, even if Kemmeter and the DSS had known of Joshua's *potential* plight as a victim of child abuse, such knowledge "neither caused the child's problem, worsened it, or made it more likely to occur." Although the authors of the Bill of Rights fully realized that free citizens faced dangers, "they concluded that these privately created perils, unlike those that could be inflicted by the government, were not of constitutional concern." The violence inflicted on Joshua by his father, although undeniably horrific, did not equal a violation of the child's constitutional rights.

These arguments were supported in an amicus curiae brief submitted by a coalition of organizations representing state and local governments that consisted of the National Association of Counties, Council of State Governments, U.S. Conference of Mayors, National Conference of State Legislatures, National League of Cities, and International City Management Association. The brief expressed their concern that a ruling in favor of Joshua would "vastly expand the liability of state and local governments" in constitutional rights violations alleged by individual citizens. Further, they feared that a favorable ruling would empower the federal courts to intervene in cases of child abuse and other family law issues that are "the recognized province of state and local governments." There can be no "federal common law of social work" curtailing the discretionary authority of state and local entities to address the problem of child abuse or threatening litigation "every time a tragedy occurs." Nor should federal courts be turned into "alternative and highly inappropriate domestic relations forums." A Supreme Court holding that knowledge of a risk to citizens' safety creates a constitutional duty to protect would do nothing less than "extend the reach of the Due Process Clause in a revolutionary manner" — one that would cripple the ability of state and local governments to function. The limited resources available to these entities require police, fire, and child welfare departments to assign priorities among various risks to the population on a daily basis. Establishing a government's liability based on agencies' knowledge that such risks exist would mean that any failure to provide adequate protection from them would expose the agencies to innumerable lawsuits. Diverting funds to litigation and damages would drain resources away from state social services, ironically diminishing their capacity to address the real and pressing problem of child abuse. Filing their own amici curiae briefs in support of the Winnebago County DSS were the U.S. deputy solicitor joined by the solicitor general and the assistant attorney general, the states of New York, Connecticut, Maryland, Oregon, Pennsylvania, and Wisconsin, and the National School Boards Association.

On the afternoon of November 2, 1988, oral arguments in *DeShaney v. Winnebago County* were presented in the U.S. Supreme Court. Later, First recalled being "very, very nervous for our side" as the previous day he and Sullivan were "sitting there and he's like cramming," circumstances that First admitted he had found most unsettling. When they arrived at the Court on the scheduled morning, the attorney recalled thinking that his partner was not as "confident, relaxed, and ready to go" as First would have preferred, and that this had made him extremely anxious. As he watched the proceedings he paid close attention to the individual actors involved, trying to read their faces, gestures, and body language in order to gauge the success of his partner's arguments.

When his time came before the Court, Sullivan began by precisely circumscribing the scope of the issue Joshua's case presented to the justices. The attorney took care to stress that the circumstances of Joshua's case were very particular, and he was arguing for the state's duty to act only in this "exquisitely narrow" context. The boy and his mother were not arguing that the Constitution inflicted a duty on the states to prevent all harm to all people, nor did they have a duty to protect all children. There is one, and only one circumstance, Sullivan asserted, where an affirmative duty exists, and that is when the child is at home — "the door is closed to the world and his natural protectors . . . become his predators and the child has no other protection." Because of the existing, extensive relationship between the state of Wisconsin and the DeShaney family — the "enmeshment" of these two entities — the state had already put itself in the position of acting as the child's protector and, having received "abundant actual knowledge" that Joshua was now in extreme danger in his father's home, the Winnebago County DSS had an affirmative duty to save him. (Sullivan's unusual term "enmeshment" appeared to have puzzled the chief justice, as he can be heard muttering the word under Sullivan's voice on the audio recording of the proceedings.) What had happened to Joshua was not only tragic, Sullivan argued, it also represented a matter now being brought appropriately before the nation's

High Court. The Court had already recognized, Sullivan continued, that the Constitution applies when a state removes a child from his parents; the rights of parenthood cannot be terminated except through due process of the law. Other constitutional rights, such as the right to bodily integrity, had also been recognized by the Court and were applicable to Joshua's case.

Here Chief Justice William Rehnquist interrupted to remind Sullivan that such constitutional protections had always been defined as being against violation by a state entity. "We've never held that right applies in a private harm," he asserted. Sullivan replied that the rights of the parents had been recognized and so should the rights of the child, an answer that only served to confuse the discussion since it muddied the issue of *from whom* Joshua was now claiming constitutional protection. For the chief justice, the pertinent question was whether the constitution protected Joshua from his father's violence, but Sullivan's argument indicated that the boy also enjoyed protection against the actions of the state. Amid the confusion Justice Sandra Day O'Connor introduced the point that previous Court rulings finding an affirmative duty on the part of the state to protect individuals' safety had not applied to private settings but rather only to institutions such as prisons and mental institutions where the state had already deprived the individual of his or her liberty. "This is certainly a step far beyond that you're asking us to take," she asserted. O'Connor then asked Sullivan whether imposing an affirmative duty on social welfare services outside of the institutional context would have a deterrent effect on states' willingness to provide such services to populations in need of them. In response, Sullivan noted that the Court's recent opinions in both *Daniels* and *Davidson* (see Chapter 4) had already held that not all negligent conduct by the state triggers Section 1983 action but had also "reserved for another occasion" the drawing of the line indicating when a state's affirmative duty to provide protective services began. "This may well be the occasion," he suggested to the justices.

Justice William Brennan then reminded Sullivan that he had yet to persuade the Court that Joshua actually had an entitlement to protection under Wisconsin law. The justice seemed to be referring to the *Roth* argument, outlined in the petitioners' brief, that state services can, in certain circumstances, become a constitutional entitlement. The attorney replied that the Fourteenth Amendment's due process clause provided the entitlement given the extreme circumstances in Joshua's case. The justices questioned Sullivan regarding the sufficiency of the Wisconsin statutes applicable to Joshua's situation and whether that state's standard of "mere negligence" could be met by the facts of this case. Justice Harry Blackmun helpfully added that the child had been severely injured, therefore he had been in a situation of extreme danger, and the state had put him there (supposing that the state did in fact know that the danger existed). Justice Blackmun's prompts seemed to be leading Sullivan more precisely toward an explicit articulation of the *Roth* argument: "I wonder why you aren't arguing it?" he finally asked Sullivan. "Maybe this [argument] is a step ahead, but it doesn't shock me as much as it shocks my brethren," the justice added.

Justice John Paul Stevens sought further clarification here, asking Sullivan to specify *when* the constitutional violation occurred, and of what it consisted. The attorney answered that the violation occurred not when Joshua was returned to his father after his initial hospital stay, but rather the very next time Kemmeter had observed signs of child abuse. He pointed out that the social worker had made a written promise to the family court that she would reactivate proceedings to remove Joshua should there be further evidence of abuse. But Justice Antonin Scalia wondered if the deprivation of Joshua's rights occurred because the child had been safe under state custody (while he had been hospitalized) and then had been returned to a dangerous home. In response, Justice Stevens pointed out that the state itself had not placed Joshua in extreme danger; rather, it had only failed to remove him later when the state knew of the violence in the home. Justice Scalia then asked whether a state social worker, upon finding a person starving in a private home, would have an affirmative duty to provide food to that individual, an analogy that seemed to further cloud rather than clarify the question of when the state can be said to have an affirmative duty to protect a child from physical harm being perpetrated by his or her parents. Chief Justice Rehnquist reiterated that the real issue before the Court at this time was the limits the Fourteenth Amendment places on the states in regard to restricting individual liberty. "I don't see how you turn that around and derive that the state has an affirmative duty," Rehnquist added, his voice betraying some annoyance.

But Justice Brennan returned to his pursuit of Joshua's entitlements under Wisconsin law. He asked Sullivan whether it made a difference to his argument *which* agents of the state may have noted danger to a child. Would a trash collector be responsible, he wondered? Sullivan replied that, no, the agent must have a statutory obligation to protect children, and this was certainly the case in Wisconsin. "Was the Wisconsin law adequate?" Justice Brennan wondered. Here Sullivan focused directly on the *Roth* argument. "I believe the child's entitlement is to the procedural protections and the intervention" as set down in the Wisconsin Children's Code. The justices explored a bit further the differing circumstances that would determine state workers' "negligence" in carrying out statutory duties as opposed to their having "intent" to deprive a citizen of his rights. At that point Sullivan's time before the justices expired.

Mark Mingo then presented arguments on behalf of the Winnebago County DSS. He asserted, clearly and succinctly, that the Fourteenth Amendment's protection for individual "liberty" does not include a right to protective services from the state. The courts had already established this precedent, and the legislative history of the Section 1983 claim demonstrates that it was never intended to be used in the way that Joshua was asking the justices to consider, namely, to compel the state to provide protective services. Second, Mingo continued, the facts of this case failed to show any action taken by the state as would be required to make a claim for the protection of individual rights. Rather, the claim was that the state had *failed* to act. Finally, Joshua's attorneys were unsuccessful in demonstrating that the social workers had acted with deliberate indifference to Joshua's plight — the necessary "state of mind" required for invoking a Fourteenth Amendment claim. The Winnebago County social workers were simply unaware of the extent of the potential harm the child faced in his father's home. And, unlike prison guards or state mental hospital staff, they were in no position to be able to determine the danger. The Court's precedents had already established the need to prove a "heightened" standard for establishing state actors' "requisite state of mind" in holding them liable. Lowering this standard threatened to "trivialize" the Fourteenth Amendment, Mingo argued, by allowing individuals to make specious claims under its banner.

Justice O'Connor asked whether the situation would be different had the state placed Joshua in foster care. "We may well [in that instance] have a case analogous to prisons and mental institutions," the attorney replied. In such a case, the state had taken a child out of his natural surroundings and placed him in the dangerous setting. Here, however, the state had done nothing to actually increase the risk of harm Joshua faced from his father. Justice Scalia pushed Mingo to clarify what actions a social worker would have to take to meet the heightened criteria he had asserted: "What if the state returns the child to a mad criminal just released from a mental institution?" Mingo agreed that such a case may well be cause for a Section 1983 claim, but this was not Joshua's situation since the state had merely returned the boy to his original status — living with the person who had legal custody over him. And the parent's legal custody, the attorney reminded the Court, is protected by the Constitution.

"And the parent's legal custody is more important than poor Joshua's safety!" Justice Harry Blackmun suddenly interjected. "Poor Joshua!"

Justice Blackmun's utterance, which later became a dramatic line in his dissenting opinion as well as the single phrase most often associated with *DeShaney v. Winnebago County* subsequently, momentarily stopped the discussion in the Court. "Poor Joshua!" Blackmun repeated. First later recalled that the justice had leaned forward in his chair, and the young attorney was convinced that the justice "wanted to startle everybody. I think he knew the case was lost and he had to do this, he had to do this." Mark Mingo seemed momentarily unsure how to proceed. Several years later, in a series of interviews Justice Blackmun gave to Harold Hongju Koh, a Yale Law School professor who had been Blackmun's law clerk, the justice explained his response in the *DeShaney* case. The justice had tried to emphasize, he said, "what [the case] meant to this little boy who was so severely injured that he would be less than normal for the rest of his life. And it seemed to me that he was the issue in the case," a point that, to Justice Blackmun, was being hopelessly lost in the various exchanges over the particular determinants of the state's liability. "This youngster was subjected to the punishment by a brutish father, and the social service agencies knew this and did nothing about it. . . . This little boy got a bad shake and nobody seemed to be very much concerned about it. That's why I referred to 'poor Joshua.'" Justice Blackmun would later flesh out his position in his dissenting opinion in the case.

Oral argument resumed when Mark Mingo returned to the point that, according to the facts of the case, no "state action" had occurred in Joshua's case. He dismissed Sullivan's "enmeshment" theory because it failed to distinguish between private and public actors. A "bright line standard" must be maintained, the attorney argued, for distinguishing between constitutional violations actionable under Section 1983 and wrongs committed by private actors that are actionable under the common law of torts. "The Fourteenth Amendment is not to be a font of tort liability," he argued. Accepting Joshua's situation as constituting a "special relationship" for the purpose of holding the state liable wherever it had expressed a desire to protect its citizens would only "open the floodgates" to lawsuits that, given limited available resources, would result in curtailing states' ability to provide public protections at all. Mingo pointed out that the Court had previously found that the due process clause applied when states had made a deliberative decision to deprive individuals of rights. The Court's "bright line standard" must be maintained to protect social workers and other public employees such as fire and police officers who were "working on the front lines" to protect the public. The social worker in Joshua's case, the attorney asserted, had not been derelict in her statutory duties. Justice Blackmun asked about the evidence presented to the Court that she had knowledge that abuse was occurring in the home. Mingo's reply was that her only duty under state law was to launch a formal investigation when she received a report of abuse and then to relay that information to the corporation counsel so that he could decide whether to petition the family court to seek protective custody of Joshua. But, he insisted, she had never received such a report on which she could have acted; there had been only suspicions that a problem might have existed in the home.

Justice Thurgood Marshall then asked Mingo to clarify the difference between formal and informal investigations of child abuse, since the social worker's responsibility to protect the child would have been the same in either case. A formal investigation, the attorney answered, is one mandated by the state statute, and an informal investigation is one that the social worker voluntarily undertook so that she could monitor Joshua's situation. The relationship between the Winnebago County DSS and the DeShaney family had been strictly voluntary, he added. Mingo reiterated that the absence of a formal report of child abuse exempted the social worker from liability in what eventually happened to Joshua. Justice Blackmun summed up Mingo's position: "No matter how much she uncovers, there is no liability if no formal report is filed." His voice retained the sad, almost despairing tone he had used minutes earlier to comment on Joshua's plight.

Following Mark Mingo, Deputy Solicitor General Donald B. Ayers presented the federal government's view that the Fourteenth Amendment was created to place limits on states' power over individual citizens rather than to require states to take specific actions for the benefit of citizens. Ayers, a Stanford Law School graduate, had clerked for William Rehnquist twelve years earlier, and subsequent to *DeShaney* argued a large number of cases before the High Court as an attorney in private practice in Washington, D.C. He added that the area of child protection was "not crying out" for federal constitutional oversight at the time, since federal and state governments were in agreement that child protection was a service under the purview of the states, who were much better positioned to know and understand the needs of their own citizens. In this case, he asserted, the state was already doing all it could be reasonably expected to do regarding the problem of child abuse. Adding an extra layer of federal oversight, Ayers argued, would be counterproductive in addressing the problem because it would delay solutions and drain scarce resources away from state child protective services. Turning more directly to Joshua's claims, Ayers asserted that the Fourteenth Amendment was designed to protect individuals against "abuse of government power" and that such abuse must be the moving action that results in harm to the individual, which was not the case here. Rather, Joshua merely had been returned to his father because the Wisconsin statute mandated that he be returned after three days if no further custody action was taken by the state. This could not be construed as "state action" in deprivation of Joshua's constitutional rights, he argued.

Addressing the *Roth* argument that state services could be construed as individual entitlements under certain circumstances, Ayers denied that the Wisconsin child protective statutes created a substantive due process interest on Joshua's part to receive protective services. Justice Scalia noted that under the Fourteenth Amendment a state does have a duty to provide equal protection of the laws to all its citizens. Ayers replied that in this case there was no evidence that

Wisconsin had intended to provide legal protections in an unequal manner. Justice Blackmun wondered about a situation in which a state had in fact placed an affirmative duty upon a state agent and the agent had failed to uphold the duty. "We can rely on state law to provide remedies" for those situations, the attorney replied. The matter was not one requiring federal intervention.

When Ayers had finished, Justice Marshall directed Sullivan (who still had one minute remaining of his assigned time before the Court) to clearly and succinctly state Joshua's Fourteenth Amendment claim. Sullivan, seemingly somewhat taken aback by Justice Marshall's question, rather hurriedly replied that the claim consisted of the state's failure to remove Joshua from his father's home knowing he was in danger, which constituted an abuse of the state's power. Oral arguments in *DeShaney v. Winnebago County* then came to an end.

Five weeks later, on December 8, 1988, Chief Justice William Rehnquist circulated the first, very brief, draft of his majority opinion to his colleagues on the Supreme Court. "Judges and lawyers, like other humans," the chief justice wrote in his four-paragraph draft, "are moved by natural sympathy in a case like this to bend the law in order that Joshua and his mother may receive adequate compensation for the grievous harm inflicted upon them." But, he went on to say, such sympathy cannot overlook the fact that it was Joshua's father, and not the state, that had inflicted the beatings to the child. Like Judge Posner on the Seventh Circuit bench, Chief Justice Rehnquist believed that the employees of the Winnebago County Department of Social Services were forced to walk a fine line between intervening to protect a child from potential harm and being "met with charges of improperly intruding into the parent-child relationship." Although the people of Wisconsin are free to enact laws that may place legal liabilities on state agencies for failing to act in situations such as Joshua's, they "should not have it thrust upon them by this Court's distortion of the Due Process Clause of the Constitution," the chief justice declared.

Justice Stevens, who had pressed Sullivan during oral arguments to clarify his argument regarding precisely *when* the state had violated Joshua's constitutional rights, asked Chief Justice Rehnquist for three changes to his initial draft. First, he wanted clarification that the opinion being rendered had no bearing on the question of a state's constitutional duties toward individuals who "have voluntarily placed themselves in the government's care, such as patients in government hospitals or military personnel." Second, he asked the chief justice to soften his rhetoric somewhat, to the effect that judges and lawyers are moved by natural sympathy to "find a way for Joshua and his mother to receive adequate compensation for the grievous harm inflicted upon them," rather than to "bend the law" in order to receive it. Finally, he asked for a rewording to the effect that the people of Wisconsin should not have state liability thrust upon them by this Court's expansion of the Due Process Clause" rather than the Court's "distortion" of it, as Rehnquist had described it. "I suggest these latter two changes," Justice Stevens explained in his memo, "because the phrases 'bend the law' and 'distortion' seem an unnecessarily harsh slap at those who may disagree with our resolution of the novel issue this case presents." In a reply memo dated the following day, the chief justice told Stevens that he was "happy to adopt the second and third suggestions made in your letter of December 13 verbatim. I actually think they improve the opinion," he added.

Justice Stevens's first suggestion, however, had given the chief justice pause, since the question of whether the ruling would apply to individuals who had voluntarily placed themselves in the state's care was only one of several potential sets of questions that the case had not addressed. "To single out one set for a disclaimer could be misleading." As a compromise, Rehnquist offered a reworking of the paragraph to read: "Petitioners concede that the harms Joshua suffered did not occur while the State was restraining his freedom to act on his own behalf, but while he was in the custody of his natural father, who in no sense is a state actor." Apparently, the new language satisfied Justice Stevens, because he joined the majority opinion two days later; Justices O'Connor, White, Kennedy, and Scalia (in chronological order) had already joined. Justice White, who had provided the fourth vote to hear the case, signed on to the majority opinion one day after it was circulated among his colleagues on the Court. Previously he had voted to grant certiorari in order to "resolve the conflict among the Federal Courts of Appeals" on the question of whether "state welfare authorities' reckless failure to protect children from physical abuse by their parents or guardians constitutes a deprivation of liberty within the meaning of the Fourteenth Amendment." For Justice White, it seems, Joshua's lawyers had failed to make their case. Ultimately, Chief Justice Rehnquist circulated four drafts of the majority opinion.

"Nothing in the language of the Due Process Clause itself," the final text of the opinion reads, "requires the State to protect the life, liberty, and property of citizens against invasion by private actors." Echoing his assertions during oral arguments, Rehnquist continued: "The Clause is phrased as a limitation on the State's power to act, not as a guarantee of certain minimal levels of safety and security. . . . Its language cannot fairly be extended to impose an affirmative obligation on the State to ensure that those interests do not come to harm through other means." The Court roundly rejected Joshua's attorneys' argument that his case was analogous to previous court decisions concerning individuals who were held in state custody. "The *Estelle/Youngberg* analysis simply has no applicability to the present case," the chief justice wrote. "While the State may have been aware of the dangers that Joshua faced in the free world, it played no part in their creation, nor did it do anything to render him any more vulnerable to them. That the State once took temporary custody of Joshua does not alter the analysis, for when it returned him to his father's custody, it placed him in no worse position than that in which he would have been had it not acted at all." The Court also rejected that argument that the existence of the Wisconsin child welfare protection system and the DeShaney family's extensive involvement with it was a sufficient fact for establishing a "special relationship" giving rise to affirmative duties. "The most that can be said of the state functionaries in this case is that they stood by and did nothing when suspicious circumstances dictated a more active role for them." The relatively succinct opinion ends with the Court's reminder that the people of Wisconsin remained free to change tort law in their state in order to place further liabilities on child protective workers. The Fourteenth Amendment to the Constitution, however, did not provide such liabilities.

In February 1989, Joshua DeShaney was just a few weeks shy of his tenth birthday. He was living in a group home for disabled children in central Wisconsin. He did not know that he had lost his case.

"Poor Joshua!"
DeShaney v. Winnebago County
in the Court of Public Opinion

One week after oral arguments were heard in *DeShaney v. Winnebago County*, Justice Brennan circulated a memorandum to his colleagues, Justices Marshall and Blackmun. "Dear Thurgood and Harry," it read, "we three are in dissent. I'll try my hand at it. Sincerely, Bill." Among his colleagues Justice Brennan was the longest-serving justice, having been on the bench since 1956. Brennan, along with Marshall (appointed in 1967) and Blackmun (appointed in 1970), constituted the liberal wing of the Court, one that by the late 1980s had increasingly found itself casting the minority vote. After Rehnquist's first draft of the majority opinion appeared for review, Brennan sent the chief justice a memo informing him of his intent to write the dissent, a draft of which was circulated on January 16, 1989.

Justice Brennan began his dissenting opinion by taking on point-blank the majority's assertion that the state of Wisconsin had failed to act on Joshua's behalf. "The most that can be said of the state functionaries," Rehnquist had written, "is that they stood by and did nothing when suspicious circumstances dictated a more active role for them." The problem, for Justice Brennan, was one of perspective. The majority took as its starting point the supposition that there is an absence of positive rights in the Constitution; recent case law had created "no general right to basic governmental services." Thus, Wisconsin's failure to act did not constitute a violation of Joshua's rights. If the right to protection from his father's violence was not found in the Constitution, and if Joshua could not claim it, then the facts that had come before the Court detailing the extensive relationship that had existed between the State of Wisconsin and the DeShaneys could be ignored. But Justice Brennan argued that the majority's starting point was not actually the question presented by Joshua's case. "No one," the justice asserted, "has asked the Court to proclaim that, as a general matter, the Constitution safeguards positive as well as negative liberties." Donald Sullivan, in fact, had attempted to make the point in oral arguments that Joshua and his mother were not seeking such a broad entitlement from the state.

For Brennan, rather, the justices' starting point should be the fact that the State of Wisconsin, through its Department of Social Services, had already extensively involved itself in Joshua's life over a period of nearly two years. Even more importantly, for Brennan, Wisconsin had given the responsibility of protecting Joshua to DSS — to the preclusion of any other potential rescuers (either public or private) when it had become apparent that the child was being abused in his home. Rejecting the "stingy scope" the majority had given to the Court's previous holdings in *Estelle v. Gamble* (a 1976 opinion in which the Court had denied a Section 1983 claim to an inmate who sued prison officials for failing to provide adequate medical treatment for a back injury he had suffered working in the prison), Brennan argued for a "much more generous proposition that, if a State cuts off private sources of aid and then refuses aid itself, it cannot wash its hands of the harm that results from its inaction." Wisconsin had established a child welfare system "specifically designed to help children like Joshua," and had given the local departments of social services a legal duty to investigate reports of child abuse. "In this way, " he concluded, "Wisconsin law invites — indeed directs — citizens and other governmental entities to depend on local departments of social services . . . to protect children from abuse" rather than undertaking rescue actions themselves. The justice cited a number of instances in Joshua's case in which suspicions that the child was being harmed in his father's home were relayed to DSS, including reports from emergency room staff, neighbors, and police — all duly chronicled by the social worker "in detail that seems almost eerie in light of her failure to act upon it," Brennan wrote. In her case notes, Ann Kemmeter herself had acknowledged that it was up to the DSS staff, subject to the corporation counsel's approval, to "make the ultimate decision" about whether to initiate the process for removing Joshua from his home.

Given that the State of Wisconsin's system was constructed in this particular way, Brennan argued, "a private citizen, or even a person working in a government agency other than the Department, would doubtless feel her job was done as soon as she had reported her suspicions of child abuse to the Department." Thus, through the very structure of the child welfare system itself, the "State of Wisconsin has relieved ordinary citizens and governmental bodies other than the Department of any sense of obligation to do anything more than report their suspicions of child abuse to the Department. If the Department ignores or dismisses these suspicions," he added, "no one will step in to fill the gap." In other words, four-year-old Joshua was completely dependent upon the state to rescue him.

For Justice Brennan, the state had "effectively confined Joshua DeShaney within the walls of Randy DeShaney's violent home until such time as the Department took action to relieve him." He strongly differed from the majority's claim that DSS had merely returned Joshua to his home in no worse condition than he would have been having had no contact with their agency. Children like Joshua, Brennan argued, are indeed "made worse off by the existence of this program when the persons and entities charged with carrying out fail to do their jobs." As the case was now positioned (the district court's issuance of a summary judgment had precluded a jury trial), no one could know why this failure occurred. Justice Brennan, therefore, "would allow Joshua and his mother the opportunity to show that respondents' failure to help him arose, not out of the sound exercise of professional judgment that we recognized in *Youngberg* as sufficient to preclude liability . . . but from the kind of arbitrariness that we have in the past condemned." As a child, Joshua was in a unique and terrible position. Although adult victims of domestic violence sometimes have the advantage of "rescuers," children do not. The justice seemed annoyed at the majority's assertion that Joshua's case might have been different had his counsel proven that the state had denied protective services to the child because he was a "disfavored minority" and thus could claim a remedy under the Fourteenth Amendment's equal protection clause; he wrote pointedly that such a statement "will be meager comfort to Joshua and his mother." Justice Brennan concluded his draft dissent by averring that "inaction can be every bit as abusive of power as action . . . oppression can result when a State undertakes a vital duty and then ignores it."

Although he was also in the minority, Justice Blackmun preferred to take a slightly different approach to Justice Brennan's. He had already asked his clerk, Edward (Ned) Foley, to begin sketching out a separate dissenting opinion, an initial draft of which was circulated on January 30. This dissent addressed more directly the argument made by Joshua's counsel that this case followed a line of previous rulings (*Bowers, Davidson, Youngberg,* and *Estelle,* for example), in which the Court had found that prior state action can lead to a subsequent duty to act. Although the state may not have known that Joshua would be severely injured by his father at the time it relinquished custody of him, there was ample evidence that the state became aware *subsequently* that it had, in fact, placed the boy in severe jeopardy. Once the realization was made, however, it had failed to remove him from that danger — and herein lay the key for Justice Blackmun. Thus to hold the state liable under the particular circumstances of this case did not necessarily contradict the view that the Constitution generally does not impose upon the states a duty to protect their residents from harm. For Justice Blackmun, the majority of the Court was "simply and startlingly incorrect in stating . . . that [state agents] stood by and did nothing"; rather, the state had actively intervened and, as a consequence, the decision to return the child to his father's custody "carried with it the further duty to protect Joshua when the State later learned that its decision had placed Joshua at great risk of serious injury." Blackmun's draft ended with a passionate statement, one that came from the justice's own pen:

> Poor Joshua! Victim of repeated attacks by an irresponsible, bullying, obviously cowardly, and intemperate father, and abandoned by respondents who placed him in a dangerous predicament and who knew or learned what was going on, and yet did essentially nothing except, as the Court revealingly observes . . . "dutifully recorded these incidents in [their] files." It is a sad commentary upon American life, and constitutional principles — so full of late of patriotic fervor and proud proclamations about "liberty and justice for all," that this child, Joshua DeShaney, now is assigned to live out the remainder of his life profoundly retarded. Joshua and his mother, as petitioners here, deserve — but now are denied by this Court — the opportunity to have the facts of their case considered in the light of the constitutional protection that Section 1983 is meant to provide.

A second draft of Justice Brennan's dissent appeared to have taken a cue from Justice Blackmun's in that it substantially strengthened the point regarding the crucial issue of state action. "Through its child-protection program, the State actively intervened in Joshua's life," it now read, "and, by virtue of this intervention, acquired ever more certain knowledge that Joshua was in grave danger." In the new draft Brennan also dropped a reference to a hypothetical case in which police officers would stand by and do nothing while watching a rape take place, keeping the focus more pointedly (and more effectively) on Joshua's situation. "Today's opinion construes the Due Process Clause to permit a State to displace private sources of protection," he wrote, "and then, at the critical moment, to shrug its shoulders and turn away from the harm" that it has promised to prevent. "Because I cannot agree that our Constitution is indifferent to such indifference, I respectfully dissent," the new version concluded.

In light of these changes to Justice Brennan's draft, Ned Foley urged Justice Blackmun to replace his own discussion of the issue of state action with something new — a direct challenge to the majority's assertion that ignoring the "natural sympathy" Joshua's case invoked constituted a particular virtue on the part of the Court. Explaining that he had been deeply influenced by Yale Law School scholar Robert M. Cover's book, *Justice Accused*, Foley's changes adopted powerful language that Justice Blackmun ultimately included in his dissent (and duly credited to Cover's influence). "Like the antebellum judges who denied relief to fugitive slaves," the final version read, "the Court today claims that its decision, however harsh, is compelled by existing legal doctrine. On the contrary," he continued, "the question presented by this case is an open one, and our Fourteenth Amendment precedents may be read more broadly or more narrowly depending upon how one chooses to read them. Faced with the choice, I would adopt a 'sympathetic' reading, one which comports with dictates of fundamental justice and recognizes that compassion need not be exiled from the province of judging."

Thus, in its final iteration, Justice Blackmun's dissent captured more transparently his own profound sense that, in stubbornly adhering to the tenet that the Constitution is a "charter of negative liberties" (a position Justice Brennan's dissent had characterized as the majority's "fixation"), the nation's High Court had done a great injustice to Joshua DeShaney. Such sterile and formalistic legal reasoning, Blackmun wrote, had "infected antebellum jurisprudence" on the fugitive slave question, and likewise contaminated the majority's opinion in the present case. Justice Blackmun's passionate, rather startling words (one legal scholar characterized them as "bitter" toward the majority) — a parry to Chief Justice Rehnquist's admonition that justices must not "yield to the impulse" of their "natural sympathy" toward a battered child — would become the cause of some notoriety among jurists and academics. As *New York Times* journalist Linda Greenhouse has noted, the *DeShaney* dissent, together with subsequent minority opinions Blackmun wrote the same year in *Webster v. Reproductive Health Services* and three years later in *Planned Parenthood v. Casey*, constituted a rare display of judicial emotion through the employment of language deliberately devoid of impartiality and intended to reach out directly to readers. Legal scholar Martha Minow observed that "this is an opinion written with drama and anger." Justice Blackmun's passionate words, "Poor Joshua!" would count among the best remembered of his long career as a jurist. In the 1995 interview Blackmun gave to Harold Hongju Koh, he confessed to "embarrassing my clerks with the use of them." Blackmun also admitted to knowing full well that the stark analogy he had drawn between fugitive slave cases and four-year-old Joshua's plight "would hit hard in the solar plexus." But the justice, nearing eighty at the time of the interview, continued to stick by his words.

The correspondence Blackmun received in the wake of the Court's decision indicates that his words did hit the public precisely where the justice had aimed. Angry citizens wrote to express their outrage, and often their shock, at the majority's conclusion. "Shame on you. . . . Shame on all of us for putting up with all of you," one such angry writer admonished. (This particular rebuke seemed to sting Justice Blackmun, as he replied: "Why do you send me a nasty mailgram? I was in the dissent.") One citizen compared the opinion to those of the early twentieth century striking down state prohibitions on child labor, which also had been misguided attempts, according to the writer, to "protect the people from the State." Another called it nothing less than "the most misguided and dangerous pronouncement of the court since Dred Scott." The distressed correspondents who wrote to Justice Blackmun about the *DeShaney* opinion included attorneys, child welfare advocates, teachers, medical doctors, and parents. One Canadian woman enclosed a check for $25 "in the hope that it can be used to help [Joshua]." Even when the letters' contents indicated the writers did not fully understand the precise nature of the legal and constitutional issues Joshua's case had brought before the Court, correspondents nevertheless were clearly moved by what they had read about Joshua's story. Indeed, Justice Blackmun's sympathetic "Poor Joshua!" had touched a nerve.

The Supreme Court's opinion in *DeShaney v. Winnebago County*, along with the dissents by Justices Brennan and Blackmun, were handed down on February 22, 1989. Two days later, the Appleton, Wisconsin, *Post-Crescent* ran a story featuring Ann Kemmeter, who was "breaking a five-year silence" in response to the High Court's decision. The newspaper reporter, James Meyer, interviewed Kemmeter at her DSS office in Neenah, in the proximity of two of the agency's supervisors, Mark Quam, director of social services, and Cheryl Stelse, Kemmeter's superior in children and family services; the supervisors' presence was required reportedly "because of the possibility of further litigation." (The Supreme Court's decision had left open the possibility that Melody and Joshua could seek redress in state court.) Although the Court had not found that the social service department had violated Joshua's constitutional rights, Justice Rehnquist's opinion had been harsh toward Kemmeter and her coworkers, charging that they "stood by and did nothing when suspicious circumstances dictated a more active role for them." But Kemmeter told the Appleton newspaper that she had a "clear conscience" regarding her actions in the case. "I'm very sorry for Joshua," she said, "but the bottom line is, I'm not the one who abused him. I think it's important to understand," she continued, "that if I had felt there was trouble in the home, that something wasn't right, I'd have certainly attempted to see to it that that child got out of there." According to Meyer, Kemmeter reiterated that, under the agreement the Winnebago County DSS had with Randy DeShaney, her home visits were strictly voluntary and that, "if Randy DeShaney did not want her there, he could have demanded that she leave." The Wisconsin Children's Code, the social worker explained, "makes it extremely difficult to remove a child from the home, regardless of a social worker's suspicions." Quam concurred, asserting that the Wisconsin Children's Code "very much gives parents the right to protection from intrusion [by the state]." Kemmeter, therefore, had acted properly under the constraints of the law.

But it was not only Kemmeter's professional reputation that had been damaged by the highly public lawsuit. Quam complained that the Winnebago County DSS had been "under a 'gag order'" that had forced the media to rely on statements from the petitioners only, thereby painting an unfair picture of the entire social service agency. "We suffered more than the man who did the act," Quam told the reporter. "Ann and Cheryl . . . have been portrayed as evil monsters, evil, cruel, uncaring monsters. It's a very cruel hoax that has been played upon them." Four days later, the *Post-Crescent* ran an editorial lending its full support to Kemmeter and the DSS, calling Kemmeter "one of the best caseworkers in the Winnebago County Social Services Department." But the editorial continued with an explanation of the nature of the case that had gone before the nation's High Court, where "the Court's job, generally, is to decide on constitutional issues. It doesn't care, in a legal sense, about individual reputations or about the facts of a case. Facts are determined by juries, not by Supreme Court justices." The district court had dismissed Joshua's lawsuit in a summary judgment, and thus no jury trial had taken place in the matter. The unfortunate result, according to the *Post-Crescent*, was that Kemmeter and her colleagues in DSS had never had the opportunity to present to the public their own side of the story.

But, if Winnebago County employees were distressed at the ordeal the lawsuit had been for them, the *Milwaukee Journal* reported social workers in that Wisconsin city were "breathing a collective sigh of relief." The newspaper quoted Thomas A. Brophy, director of the social services department in Milwaukee County, as declaring "it would have been impossible for caseworkers to function in an environment where they can be sued for judgments when the family's situation could change rapidly the moment they left the home." Attorney Mark Mingo agreed, telling the newspaper that "if we had received an adverse opinion, it would have opened up a Pandora's box of liability." Similarly, the public guardian of Cook County, Illinois, Patrick Murphy, told the *Chicago Tribune* that "there are thousands and thousands of kids whose cases are investigated by state agencies for abuse." Had the Supreme Court found the state liable, "we're opening the floodgates for thousands and thousands of lawsuits." He speculated that "agencies would be taking (children) out of their homes for fear of liability." The alternative available to such children — the foster care system — was not necessarily the answer for Murphy who, according to the *Tribune*, had himself filed numerous lawsuits against the social services system in Illinois on behalf of children who had allegedly been abused in foster homes and emergency shelters.

The *Milwaukee Journal*'s editorial board, however, was not as sanguine about the positive effect of the *DeShaney* ruling on state child protection services. "The law has always recognized children as a vulnerable class deserving special protection," a March 5 editorial read, "Who, if not the state, can protect the rights of someone like Joshua who cannot protect himself?" In ruling that Joshua did not have a constitutional right to state protection from his father's violence, the Supreme Court had also declared that states were free to enact their own laws holding agents of the state liable for failure to provide that protection, and the *Journal* now urged the Wisconsin legislature to take just such action: "Surely there is a way to draft a law that improves the accountability of public employees in well-documented cases of abuse," the editors posited, "without inviting unnecessary intrusions into family relationships." The editors ventured further that such legal changes would result in more sound public policy, speculating that "it's cheaper to hire more social workers and underwrite more foster homes than to pay for the lifetime institutionalization of brain-damaged youngsters." The Milwaukee newspaper also published a number of readers' letters expressing outrage over the High Court's decision in Joshua's case.

For its part, the Wisconsin Bureau of Children, Youth, and Families did not wait for state legislators to act. Within days of the Court's ruling the bureau announced a new initiative of its own. A state child welfare official told the Appleton *Post-Crescent* that new uniform standards for training child protection workers were being promoted for adoption by every county in Wisconsin. Under the present arrangement, according to Linda Hisgen, "each of the state's seventy-two counties now does it differently, and so does each social worker in each county." The new program, originally designed by a North-Carolina–based organization called Action for Child Protection, approached the duties of child protection workers "from a perspective of being totally focused on the degree of risk to the child." Wisconsin child welfare officials were optimistic that the new initiative would help to standardize practices employed by child protection workers throughout the state.

At the national level, Tom Birch, counsel for the National Child Abuse Coalition headquartered in Washington, D.C., told reporters his organization approved of the Supreme Court's ruling in the *DeShaney* case. Social workers, he explained, were now alleviated of their fears of being sued — and this would result in better protections for children. "When [social workers] are not held to the high standard of liability this case imposes," Birch said, "they will have the flexibility they need to protect the child when appropriate." *USA Today* quoted an attorney for the National School Boards Association as finding relief in the High Court's decision as well. "We would have been in real trouble" had Joshua won, she said. Likewise, Benna Ruth Solomon of the State and Local Legal Center in Washington, D.C., told *Time* magazine that "a contrary ruling would have seriously affected programs and budgetary priorities." The floodgates, for now at least, remained closed.

In the months following the *DeShaney* decision social workers considered its implications for their profession. A 1990 essay in *Social Work*, the organ of the National Association of Social Workers, warned that despite its refusal to find a constitutional claim for Joshua, the ruling offered "cold comfort" for child protection workers, noting that liability may still attach if caseworkers make an arbitrary decision not to help a child they knew was being abused based on the child's ethnic or racial origin. Nor did the ruling prevent legislatures from easing the way for plaintiffs seeking to sue public child welfare agencies and their employees in state courts. Nevertheless, a popular child welfare training manual published the following year noted — incorrectly — that the Supreme Court had "absolved Winnebago County, indicating that public officials were not obliged to save children from privately inflicted harm." This characterization, of course, failed to distinguish between federal lawsuits and those brought in the states.

Within a few weeks of the Court's decision nationally syndicated columnists had chimed into the public discourse surrounding the *DeShaney* opinion. Echoing the majority's language, Washington, D.C.–based journalist James J. Kilpatrick counseled his readers that in "the midst of our Dickensian emotion over the beaten child and a bumbling bureaucracy, let us keep a clear eye on the law in this case," which had been in fact correctly decided by the nation's High Court according to him. He compared the situation of the Wisconsin DSS workers to that of Washington, D.C., police officers who must not be held liable for failing to prevent homicides in certain areas of the city "that have become virtual war zones in the battle against drug dealers." Similarly, Ellen Goodman, another nationally syndicated columnist, supported the Court's decision. "I find myself in rare agreement with a conservative court," Goodman wrote in the *Boston Globe*. "It was not the state or caseworker that destroyed Joshua's future. It was his father. If there is an injustice, it's that Randy DeShaney spent less than two years in jail, while Joshua will spend his life in an institution." Goodman continued that, had the Court decided in favor of Joshua, "in our lawsuit-happy world, any firefighter, police officer, ambulance driver, or social worker might have been sued by a citizen who claimed the right of protection." Within such a scenario, state budgets would become depleted and already scarce resources for vital social services would dry up. Mark Mingo agreed, writing to remind the *American Bar Association Journal* that "difficult and often overwhelming burdens [are] placed upon state social workers" such as his clients in the Winnebago County DSS.

Taking a broader perspective, the *New York Times* Supreme Court correspondent Linda Greenhouse placed Joshua's case within a larger context of growing conservatism on the Supreme Court, the product of judicial appointments made during the two administrations of President Ronald Reagan. (Justices Sandra Day O'Connor, Antonin Scalia, and Anthony Kennedy were Reagan appointees, and William Rehnquist was elevated to chief justice in 1986, having served as an associate justice since 1972.) In a July column, written after the closing of the 1988 term, she asserted that the previous year had marked a "decided shift in the Court's orientation" characterized by a "polarization and conservative dominance" among the nine justices, and included *DeShaney v. Winnebago County* in her summary of the year's most important decisions. For many contemporary Court watchers the decision, which promoted a narrow scope for the constitutional claims that individual citizens could make under Section 1983, signaled a decisive turn to the political right.

Legal scholars soon weighed in on the significance of *DeShaney* as well. Harvard Law School scholar Laurence Tribe, who had clerked for Supreme Court Justice Potter Stewart from 1967 to 1968 and was himself a well-established veteran presenting arguments before the Supreme Court, charged that in deciding against Joshua's case the

Court had demonstrated not only a lack of "heart" but faulty "peripheral vision" as well. Speaking at a commencement at the New York University School of Law in May 1989 (and responding to a lecture delivered earlier that month at Harvard by Justice Scalia), Tribe supported the position of the dissenting justices that the majority had focused on the wrong question. The State of Wisconsin had created a system, Tribe charged, in which only the social services bureaucracy could have rescued Joshua from his father's violent home; it was against Wisconsin law for "well-meaning citizens to barge into a private home in response to a child's cries for help." But, having created a structure in which Joshua was dependent on social workers alone for his safety, the Court had failed to find that the state had an affirmative duty to ensure that protection when "social service bureaucrats knew all about those awful beatings." Tribe supported Justice Blackmun's call for a "sympathetic reading" of the Constitution that would construe Joshua's right to protection under its umbrella. "To say that we will not break or bend the law simply out of sympathy for a victim like Joshua, or out of distaste for his attacker, is exactly right," Tribe asserted. "But to say that our idea of 'law' is to be constructed with straightedge and compass, without sympathy and compassion, is *dead wrong*." Tribe focused on the *DeShaney* decision in another address that month, given before the New York City Bar Association. Borrowing imagery from quantum physics, Tribe accused the majority of being locked into a "stilted premodern paradigm" that construed the law as a kind of well-ordered machine, much as seventeenth-century Newtonians had envisioned the natural universe. Within such a mechanistic universe, the Court had taken the reality of child abuse as an "unfortunate, yet external, ante-legal and pre-political fact of our society." The Court preferred to remain a detached and dispassionate observer of domestic violence, only stepping in if it were the state itself dealing blows to a child. According to Tribe, the majority had asked only "did the State of Wisconsin beat up that child?" It had not inquired whether the state had in fact already acted by "warping the legal landscape so that it in effect deflected the assistance otherwise available to Joshua DeShaney." It was only the dissenters who had been able to step away from such a rigid and obsolete paradigm, a move Tribe likened to that of more recent physicists who had reconceptualized the universe as curved space — a complete paradigm shift that enabled the dissenters to see new possibilities in the scope of civil rights protections afforded by the Constitution.

The legal path was already there, Tribe suggested, pointing to the Court's own 1971 opinion, *Boddie v. Connecticut.* In this case the justices had struck down a state law requiring divorcing couples to pay a filing fee. An indigent couple had successfully challenged the statute, arguing that the State of Connecticut held a monopoly on the means of obtaining a divorce; therefore preventing poor people's access to the process was an unconstitutional violation of their rights to due process. No state action had been directed at particular individuals, but the Court nevertheless found for Boddie because "it was the legal structure itself . . . that had isolated the person from the fulfillment of an important need." Likewise, for Tribe, "the governmental act in *DeShaney* that had isolated Joshua . . . was not a force directed at Joshua personally" but instead resulted from "the simple juxtaposition of Wisconsin law and his personal situation." Like the indigent Boddie, Joshua was a particularly vulnerable individual dependent upon a legal structure created by the state. "We may all be engulfed by, and dependent upon, the structure of the law," Tribe wrote, "but we are not all rendered equally vulnerable by it." Abused children, arguably, are the most vulnerable of all.

Differential vulnerability was also central to the University of Houston Law Center's Laura Oren, whose critique of the *DeShaney* opinion appeared the following year in the *North Carolina Law Review.* For Oren, the Court had mistakenly abstracted the case from its particularized context of family violence. The majority's rhetoric of individualism had relied on "all the positive associations of freedom" that Americans associate with the notion of keeping the state out of the private family; maintaining a bright line between private and public custody spheres guarantees citizens that the courts will "prevent the state from breaking into our homes and beating us up." But, for Oren, such language only serves to "create a false equivalency between people, predicaments, and liberties that are not truly alike. Even laissez-faire ideologues," she charged, "have long recognized that dependent children (and, at one time, women) do not fit the model of free agents acting in a free society." Oren suggested that one avenue of relief for child abuse victims lay in the development of "state of mind" requirements triggering affirmative constitutional duties *within the specific context of* child protection services. It would be possible, she argued, to develop a standard that would allow broad discretion to social workers in carrying out their duties and at the same time setting a "rigorous standard of culpability" to ensure protections for child victims. Oren feared, however, that the *DeShaney* majority drawing a rigid line between state and private actions would cut off opportunities to develop this area in the courts.

The *DeShaney* opinion set off a flurry of legal scholarship critical of the Court's reliance on the supposition that the Constitution afforded only "negative rights." In 1990 Susan Bandes of the DePaul University College of Law, for example, offered an extensive critique in the *Michigan Law Review*. Dualistic concepts such as state action and state in-action, private action and public action, or negative rights and positive rights, Bandes argued, "tell us little which will assist in making difficult choices about the role of government." This is because such concepts do not exist in the absence of values, a set of reference points by which we can make sense of them. Mechanistic formulae that purport to apply such concepts — although claiming to exist in a normatively neutral space, outside the realm of value choices — in reality, for Bandes, do in fact represent value choices: "To condemn only physical or tangible interference, to prefer the status quo, to protect certain entitlements while leaving the means for satisfying others to the vagaries of the open market," are all choices with moral implications. The *DeShaney* Court, according to Bandes, "chose a rough form of justice" for Joshua — one that will "continue to protect the injustices inherent in the current order" — yet the Court mistakenly believed itself to be acting outside the realm of value choices. The view of the Constitution as solely a "negative document" had led the Court to concern itself with "the elusive and ultimately irrelevant distinction between 'freedom from and freedom to.'" For Bandes, the really crucial question should be, "what must we have in order to be free?" The answers to that question, she argued, would signify those things that the Constitution protects. Victims of child abuse, from this perspective, needed the protections to their physical security afforded by an active state.

Akhil Reed Amar and Daniel Widawsky took up Justice Blackmun's analogy of Joshua's case to that of antebellum fugitive slaves and subjected it to further analysis. Writing in the *Harvard Law Review* in 1992, they argued that the Thirteenth Amendment's prohibitions on slavery and involuntary servitude afforded affirmative protections for abused children because the position of such children was analogous to that of slaves. "Like an antebellum slave," the authors asserted, "an abused child is subject to near total domination and degradation by another person, and is treated more as a possession than as a person. . . . And just as antebellum states enforced the legal rights of masters to physical control over their slaves, today's states continued to enforce the legal rights of parents to physical control over their children." When such lawfully granted physical control over children crosses the line into child abuse, a parent "perverts his coercive authority" and treats the child "not as a person but as a chattel, acting as if he had title over rather than trusteeship on behalf of the child." The Thirteenth Amendment's prohibition on slavery compels the state to put a stop to its practice regardless of the context in which it occurs. That a person's enslavement takes place in a private home is of no relevance under the amendment; the state must nevertheless take action to stop it. The state, in fact, had already taken action in that Randy DeShaney had received custody of Joshua through an action of the state; his biological mother, Melody, did not have custody. Thus, biological parenthood was not necessarily destiny, and "the state, through its family law, chooses who shall have custody of a ward. . . . Custody," they continued, "is a *legal* concept, shaped and enforced by the state." Nineteenth-century slave children, after all, were freed from their masters by the Thirteenth Amendment even when their masters were also their biological fathers. Amar and Widawsky asserted further that the very specificity of the Thirteenth Amendment's prohibitions of slavery (as opposed to the Fourteenth's malleable due process protections) and the extension of these prohibitions to physically abusing children avoided the nightmarish scenario painted by the *DeShaney* Court in which state agents such as police officers, firefighters, and emergency medical technicians would become liable for failing to prevent catastrophes.

But, if legal scholars offered no shortage of alternative legal theories supporting a finding in favor of Joshua DeShaney, the fact remained that he had lost his case in the nation's High Court. Further, the Supreme Court's ruling that Joshua had no constitutional claim to state protection from his father's violence effectively barred other challenges from being heard as well. Two weeks after the opinion in *DeShaney v. Winnebago County* was handed down, Linda Greenhouse of the *New York Times* reported that the Court "in a series of terse, unsigned orders" had tossed back to the lower courts eight other cases dealing with the question of whether the Constitution imposes a "duty to rescue" on public officials. (When the Court had agreed to hear Joshua's case, it had put on hold similar cases pending its decision.) In two of the cases, the Court vacated lower court rulings that had been favorable toward plaintiffs suing public officials. One involved a Philadelphia student who had successfully sued a school district for damages after she had been molested by a teacher; the second case concerned a citizen who had won a suit against the City of New Kensington, Pennsylvania, stemming from an incident in which city police responding to reports of a bar fight had not stopped a beating that had resulted in a patron's death. However, in denying review to a Georgia case the Court let stand a lower court's finding that permitted a suit against child welfare officials who had failed to prevent the beating of a two-year-old girl at the hands of her foster parents; the beating had resulted in the child falling into an irreversible coma. Oral arguments in *DeShaney* had, in fact, indicated that the justices saw increased responsibility for the states for the welfare of children placed in the foster care system than it did for children like Joshua who were living with their legal custodians at the time of their victimization.

Further adjudication of questions concerning state responsibility for abused children would take place in state, not federal, courts. Marcia Robinson Lowry of the American Civil Liberties Union Children's Rights Project told the *Chicago Tribune* that, although Joshua's case represented an attempt to "open up the law" on the federal level, children's advocates only rarely brought cases to federal courts, so the impact of the Court's decision on her organization's work would be minimal. Years later her colleague Christopher Hansen agreed, noting that a great deal of child advocacy work actually took place in local and family courts. Looking back on *DeShaney v. Winnebago County*, Curry First did not see great changes for child advocacy, either. "The sad part is before this decision, the government's actual conduct in this area wasn't good. . . . So I don't think things necessarily slid down that drastically." Nevertheless, First saw the possibility that although state child protection agencies may have issued a sigh of relief at the High Court's ruling in 1989, they also may have subsequently become much more aware of their legal responsibilities regarding victims of abuse.

The evidence from child welfare professionals, however, was mixed. In 1993, for example, the journal *Social Work* reported that a recent national study had revealed a 60 percent noncompliance rate with mandated reporting laws among child welfare professionals. According to Elizabeth D. Hutchinson, reasons for noncompliance included an unwillingness to disrupt the "therapeutic alliance" between social workers and their clients, hesitancy to become involved in the legal system (possibly because of the vagueness of many states' reporting statutes as well as the extensive commitment of time and effort required), erroneous fears of being held liable if accusations of abuse are not substantiated, and a lack of actual benefits to their clients, since the existing services provided to victims by the state were often ineffective anyway. Similarly, in 1999 Daniel J. Sonkin and Douglas Scott Liebert noted that confusion continued to exist among mental health workers regarding their states' legal reporting requirements for suspected child abuse. The authors identified several factors that served to create a dilemma for mental health services providers when they confronted cases in which they suspected abuse, including risks to their relationships with their clients, uncertainty about interpreting possible signs of abuse, lack of familiarity with the appropriate legal standards and procedures to follow, and the ethical dilemmas inherent when providers take on dual roles as both therapists and investigators. Conversely, Douglas J. Besharov and Lisa A. Lauman argued in a 1996 issue of *Society* that the *overreporting* of child abuse constituted a substantial problem facing child welfare professionals. The authors pointed to a 1993 survey by the National Committee to Prevent Child Abuse that found only 34 percent of reports of suspected abuse were substantiated. Such overreporting, the authors warned, was overwhelming the scarce resources available for child protective agencies and therefore minimizing the chances that children who were really at risk would be helped. They pointed to the emergence of organizations such as Victims of Child Abuse Laws, a group dedicated to lobbying for reforms in child welfare agency procedures as well as changes in state and federal laws that were attempting to reduce the incidence of unfounded accusations.

Ann Kemmeter continued her career as a social worker in the Winnebago County DSS until her retirement, after nearly thirty-eight years, in January 2005. Shortly after Joshua's final beating she had taken on a position as a social work liaison with the Neenah police department, which honored her years of service with a plaque upon her retirement. "Ann's work ethic as well as her skills in dealing with abused children is unmatched," the *Post-Crescent* quoted Neenah detective David Rueth as saying. Asked about the *DeShaney* case from the perspective of nearly twenty years, Kemmeter told reporter Michael King that the High Court had supported the lower courts' dismissal of the case "because we cannot predict people's behaviors. As tragic as it was for Joshua," she continued, "I think in the end, we as public employees benefitted from that final decision." Mark Quam reiterated his opinion from previous years that the lawsuit had been "very unfair. You're not in a position in protective services where you can protect everyone. It was a textbook example of how you were supposed to process a case. It was just very unfortunate," he added. The notoriety of Joshua's case, it seems, cast a long shadow over the Winnebago County DSS and the individuals who worked there.

Donald Sullivan, however, had a markedly different perspective on the outcome of Joshua's case. He had expressed his considerable dismay over the Court's decision in 1989, telling *USA Today* that he could "feel the unspeakable terror these kids face when they are abused . . . and I am angry." Years later, he remained critical that Americans "say that we care about kids, we say that we put kids first, [but] talk is cheap." Sullivan had come to see the High Court's opinion as "the collective decision of our society at a given moment in time. I don't have to like it, but I can understand it." Sullivan remained optimistic that change was still possible. "Somewhere down the road," he asserted, "somebody is going to win the *DeShaney* case, and all of us, all of us, will be better off." He likened the *DeShaney* opinion to the nineteenth-century decision upholding racial segregation, *Plessy v. Ferguson*, and he predicted it would eventually be overturned by the Supreme Court just as the Court had overturned de jure segregation in *Brown v. Board of Education.*

More than fifteen years after the Supreme Court handed down its opinion in *DeShaney v. Winnebago County*, legal scholars, child welfare experts, and historians continue to examine and debate its meaning for American families, for children's rights, and for the role of the state in modern U.S. society. Joshua DeShaney remains in a group home for severely disabled adults in central Wisconsin.

1962   The *Journal of the American Medical Association* publishes its watershed report, "The Battered Child Syndrome."

1974   Congress passes the Child Abuse and Treatment Act, providing funds for state programs for detecting and preventing child abuse.

1977   Wisconsin amends its child protection laws, known as the Children's Code. In section 940.201, "Abuse of Children" is designated as a Class E felony.

1979   President Jimmy Carter establishes the Office of Domestic Violence. Joshua DeShaney is born in Cheyenne, Wyoming. Twenty-one months later, his parents are divorced. Melody DeShaney surrenders custody to Joshua's father Randy, who relocates to central Wisconsin.

1980   Congress passes the Adoption Assistance and Welfare Act, mandating that state child welfare agencies make "reasonable efforts" to preserve family units before removing children when abuse is suspected.

1981   Congress cuts the budget of the Adoption Assistance and Welfare Act by 21 percent.

1982   The Winnebago County Department of Social Services (DSS) receives its first report that Joshua DeShaney is being physically abused by his father.

1983   Joshua DeShaney makes his first trip to the emergency room of the Theda Clark Regional Medical Center in Neenah in January. The State of Wisconsin takes temporary custody of Joshua but releases him to his father the next day. DSS and Randy DeShaney enter into a voluntary agreement. Over the next eleven months, Joshua is seen at hospital emergency rooms three times and on home visits child protective worker Ann Kemmeter notes numerous injuries on the child's body in her files. Police are called to the home for domestic disturbances six times.

1984   On March 7 Kemmeter arrives for a home visit but is told Joshua is sleeping. The following evening he is brought to the hospital in a coma and undergoes emergency neurosurgery. On December 10, Randy DeShaney pleads "no contest" to felony abuse charges.

1985   In February, Randy DeShaney is sentenced to four years in prison to be served consecutively. He is paroled two years and seven months later. Joshua and Melody DeShaney bring a civil suit against DSS in the federal district court in Milwaukee, charging that its failure to protect Joshua was a violation of the child's Fourteenth Amendment rights.

1986   In June, Judge John W. Reynolds grants a motion for a summary judgment, thereby precluding a jury trial. One month later, the U.S. Court of Appeals for the Seventh Circuit agrees to hear Joshua and Melody's appeal.

1987   Oral arguments in *DeShaney v. Winnebago County* are heard in January and one month later Judge Richard A. Posner issues the court's opinion against Joshua and Melody. They appeal to the U.S. Supreme Court.

1988   The Supreme Court agrees to hear the case in March. Oral arguments are presented in November.

1989   The U.S. Supreme Court rules against Joshua and Melody DeShaney, finding no state action conferring liability for violating Joshua's constitutional rights.

BIBLIOGRAPHIC ESSAY

Note from the series editors: The following bibliographical essay contains the primary and secondary sources the author consulted for this volume. We have asked all authors in the series to omit formal citations in order to make our volumes more readable, inexpensive, and appealing for students and general readers.

Joshua DeShaney's story has been told many times, in the widespread press coverage that surrounded his case as well as in law review articles analyzing the decision. The vast majority of these retellings, however, have relied on the picture presented by the Court itself in its majority opinion. As a historian, I wanted to know more, and that meant a return to the primary sources. The opinion's citation in the *United States Reports* is *DeShaney v. Winnebago County Department of Social Services*, 489 U.S. 189 (1989); it is also accessible through the online reference sources FindLaw and Lexis-Nexis. I discovered, however, that a wealth of relevant details not referred to in the opinion exists in the briefs as well as a voluminous joint appendix that includes substantial excerpts from the more than 3,700 pages of depositions and from Ann Kemmeter's case notes. The full set of briefs can be found in most law libraries as well as many university and large public libraries. A complete recording of the oral arguments can be heard by accessing the Oyez website at http:// www.oyez.org/oyez/resource/case/634; my thanks go to Jerry Goldman for permitting me to include material from the Oyez audiofile in this book. The text of the opinion is accessible at http://www.justia.us/us/489/189/case.html. An edited recording of the oral arguments, with commentary by legal scholar Peter Irons, is included in Peter Irons and Stephanie Guitton, editors, *May It Please the Court: The Most Significant Oral Arguments Made before the Supreme Court since 1955* (New York: New Press, 1993), a set that includes both audiotapes and transcripts. A standard reference work to accompany researchers' explorations into official Court documents is Bryan A. Garner, editor, *Black's Law Dictionary*, 8th ed. (St. Paul, MN: West, 2004).

A wonderful opportunity for legal historians was presented in the spring of 2004 when the papers of Justice Harry A. Blackmun became open to the public at the Manuscript Division of the Library of Congress. The collection includes transcripts from the Justice Harry A. Blackmun Oral History Project, a series of interviews conducted by Harold Hongju Koh; both the transcripts and video recordings of the interviews are available on the Library of Congress Harry A. Blackmun Papers website at http://www.loc.gov/ rr/mss/blackmun. The manuscript collection includes a case file of enlightening material pertaining to *DeShaney*, such as the justice's handwritten notes during oral arguments and memos exchanged with his law clerks as the dissenting opinion took shape. The collection also contains correspondence he received from the public concerning the opinion. Longtime *New York Times* legal reporter Linda Greenhouse has published a useful introduction to Justice Blackmun's role on the Court based on her research in this collection, *Becoming Justice Blackmun: Harry Blackmun's Supreme Court Journey* (New York: Times Books, 2005). The book Justice Blackmun cited as influencing his dissent is Robert M. Cover, *Justice Accused: Antislavery and the Judicial Process* (New Haven: Yale University Press, 1975). The dissenting opinions that, along with *DeShaney*, reveal Justice Blackmun's strong emotions appear in the cases *Webster v. Reproductive Health Services*, 492 U.S. 490 (1989) and *Planned Parenthood v. Casey*, 510 U.S. 1309 (1994).

Important cases cited in support of the plaintiffs' arguments in *DeShaney v. Winnebago County* include *Palsgraf v. the Long Island Railroad Company*, 249 NY 511 (1928); *Board of Regents v. Roth*, 408 U.S. 564 (1972); *Spence v. Staras*, 507 F. 2d 554 (1974); *Estelle v. Gamble*, 429 U.S. 97 (1976); *White v. Rochford*, 592 F. 2d 381 (1979); *Doe v. New York City Department of Social Services*, 649 F. 2d 134 (1981); *Bowers v. DeVito*, 686 F. 2d 616 (1982); *Youngberg v. Romeo*, 457 U.S. 307 (1982); *Doe v. New York City Department of Social Services*, 709 F. 2d 782 (1983); *Jensen v. Conrad*, 747 F. 2d 185 (1984); *Benson v. Cady*, 761 F. 2d 335 (1985); and *Estate of Bailey v. County of York*, 768 F. 2d 503 (1985). Important cases cited in the defendants' arguments include: *Estelle v. Gamble*, 439 U.S. 97 (1976); *Martinez v. California*, 444 U.S. 277 (1980); *Jackson v. City of Joliet*, 715 F. 2d 1200 (1983); *Daniels v. Williams*, 474 U.S. 327 (1986); *Davidson v. Cannon*, 474 U.S. 344 (1986); and *Archie v. City of Racine*, 847 F. 2d 1211 (1988).

All records and briefs for *DeShaney* in the U.S. District Court, Eastern District of Wisconsin, are housed at the National Archives and Records Administration Great Lakes Region headquarters in Chicago, Illinois. The files include Judge John W. Reynolds's ruling granting Winnebago County's request for a summary judgment. Judge Richard Posner's opinion for the U.S. Court of Appeals in the Seventh Circuit is published in the *Federal Reporter* at 812 F. 2d 298 (1987). Other records and briefs pertaining to *DeShaney* in the federal appeals court are located at the Everett McKinley Dirksen U.S. Courthouse in Chicago.

This study has included the criminal case that resulted from Joshua DeShaney's abuse. I obtained several reports through the Records Division of the Oshkosh Police Department and the Wisconsin Department of Justice Crime Information Bureau. A large body of material, including medical and police reports, trial transcripts, and other records pertaining to the criminal case are on file at the Winnebago County Courthouse in Oshkosh and available through the Office of the Clerk of Courts. I would like to especially thank Diane M. Fremgen and her staff for their generous assistance in helping me to locate and access these materials.

Oral history can serve as an extraordinary methodological tool, and I am extremely grateful to the people who were willing to discuss *DeShaney v. Winnebago County* with me in person, through telephone interviews, and via traditional and email correspondence. I have gained a far more nuanced sense of the story and the actors involved through my discussions with these individuals. In the interest of fairness and accuracy, I sought out interviews with as many individuals concerned with the case as I was able to locate; several politely declined my request. I would like to thank especially Joshua's attorneys, Donald Sullivan and Curry First, Winnebago County's attorney Mark J. Mingo, Detectives Michael Novotny and Keith Nelson, Christopher Hansen, Senior Staff Counsel at the American Civil Liberties Union and formerly with the ACLU's Children's Rights Project, and William Glaberson of the *New York Times* for their generosity, interest, and helpfulness. Glaberson's sympathetic profile of Melody DeShaney is included in "Determined to Be Heard: Four Americans and Their Journeys to the Supreme Court," *New York Times Magazine* (October 2, 1988): 32–40. Tape recordings, transcripts, and notes of all interviews I conducted remain in my possession.

Historians have yet to fully evaluate the role of the Rehnquist Court in modern U.S. history. A number of significant works by nonhistorians helped me to assess *DeShaney v. Winnebago County* in terms of the makeup of the Court as a whole. These include books by legal scholars Edward Lazarus, *Closed Chambers: The Rise, Fall, and Future of the Modern Supreme Court* (New York: Penguin Books, 1999); Mark Tushnet, *A Court Divided: The Rehnquist Court and the Future of Constitutional Law* (New York: W. W. Norton, 2005); and Tinsley E. Yarbrough, *The Rehnquist Court and the Constitution* (New York: Oxford University Press, 2000). Researchers new to the topic of the Supreme Court will find an invaluable starting place in two key reference works, Kermit L. Hall, editor, *The Oxford Companion to the Supreme Court* (New York: Oxford University Press, 1992) and Melvin I. Urofsky, editor, *The Supreme Court Justices: A Biographical Dictionary* (New York: Garland, 1994).

The history of domestic violence in the United States has not been extensively studied but several important works have done much to illuminate the issue in the past. Most valuable among these are Linda Gordon, *Heroes of Their Own Lives: The Politics and History of Family Violence* (New York: Viking, 1988) and Elizabeth Pleck, *Domestic Tyranny: The Making of American Social Policy against Family Violence from Colonial Times to the Present* (Urbana: University of Illinois Press, 2004). Susan Brownmiller's *Against Our Will: Men, Women, and Rape* (New York: Simon and Schuster, 1975) is a pathbreaking feminist analysis of family violence.

By contrast, child welfare policy and institutions and child-saving movements have garnered a great deal of attention from historians and social scientists. Here I offer just a sample of the works that can be counted among the most important for researchers interested in understanding the broad picture of this history: Robert H. Bremner, *Children and Youth in America: A Documentary History* (Cambridge: Harvard University Press, 1971); Fred R. Johnson, "The Field of Public Welfare," *Annals of the American Academy of Political and Social Science* 145, Part I (September 1929); E. Marguerite Gane, "A Decade of Child Protection," *Annals of the American Academy of Political and Social Science* 212 (November 1940): 153–158; Barbara J. Nelson, *Making an Issue of Child Abuse: Political Agenda Setting for Social Problems* (Chicago: University of Chicago Press, 1984); Kriste Lindenmeyer, *"A Right to Childhood": The U.S. Children's Bureau and Child Welfare, 1912–1946* (Urbana: University of Illinois Press, 1997); Robyn Muncy, *Creating a Female Dominion in American Reform, 1890–1935* (New York: Oxford University Press, 1991); Sonya Michel, *Children's Interests/Mothers' Rights: The Shaping of America's Child Care Policy* (New Haven: Yale University Press, 1999); Theda Skocpol, *Protecting Soldiers and Mothers: The Political Origins of Social Policy in the United States* (Cambridge: Harvard University Press, 1992); Joan Gittens, *Poor Relations: The Children of the State in Illinois, 1818–1990* (Urbana: University of Illinois Press, 1994); and Timothy A. Hasci, *Second Home: Orphan Asylums and Poor Families in America* (Cambridge: Harvard University Press, 1997).

Daniel J. Walkowitz's *Working with Class: Social Workers and the Politics of Middle Class Identity* (Chapel Hill: University of North Carolina Press, 1999); Michael Katz, *In the Shadow of the Poorhouse: A Social History of Welfare in America* (New York: Basic Books, 1986); Linda Gordon, *Pitied but Not Entitled: Single Mothers and the History of Welfare, 1890–1935* (New York: Free Press, 1994); and Lela B. Costin, Howard Jacob Karger, and David Stoesz, *The Politics of Child Abuse in America* (New York: Oxford University Press, 1996) all focus more directly on the development of the social work profession. Although Darlene Clark Hines's *Black Women in White: Racial Conflict and Cooperation in the Nursing Profession, 1880–1950* (Bloomington: Indiana University Press, 1989) does not focus on social work per se, black visiting nurses were often the only social welfare professionals serving African American communities and thus her study is enlightening. Each of these scholarly analyses made significant contributions to my understanding of this topic.

For the perspectives of child protective workers themselves from the 1970s through the 1990s, I consulted Vincent DeFrancis and Carroll L. Lucht, *Child Abuse Legislation in the 1970s*, rev. ed. (Denver, CO: American Humane Association Children's Division, 1974); Lela B. Costin and Charles A. Rapp, editors, *Child Welfare: Policies and Practice*, 1st, 2nd, and 3rd eds. (New York: McGraw Hill, 1972, 1979, and 1984); Lela B. Costin, Cynthia J. Bell, and Susan W. Downs, editors, *Child Welfare: Policies and Practice* (New York: Longman, 1991); Mark W. Fraser, Peter J. Pecora, and David A. Haapala, *Families in Crisis: The Impact of Intensive Family Preservation Services* (New York: de

Gruyter, 1991); Seth C. Kalichman, *Mandated Reporting of Suspected Child Abuse: Ethics, Law, and Policy* (Washington, DC: American Psychological Association, 1999); Daniel Jay Sonkin and Douglas Scott Liebert, "Legal and Ethical Issues in the Treatment of Multiple Victimization Child Treatment," in R. Rossman and M. Rosenberg, editors, *Multiple Victimization Child Maltreatment: Clinical and Research Perspectives* (New York: Hayworth, 1999); and Peter H. Rossi, John R. Schuerman, and Stephen Budde, *Understanding Child Maltreatment Decisions and Those Who Make Them* (Chicago: Chapin Hall Center for Children, June 1996). I would like to thank Katherine Bullard for bringing the work of the Chapin Hall Center for Children to my attention.

Social work professionals' assessments of *DeShaney v. Winnebago County* can be found in Elizabeth D. Hutchinson, "Mandatory Reporting Laws: Child Protective Case Finding Gone Awry?" *Social Work* 38 (January 1993): 56–63; Ronald K. Bullis, "Cold Comfort from the Supreme Court: Limited Liability Protection for Social Workers," *Social Work* 35 (July 1990): 364–366; Rudolph Alexander, Jr., "The Legal Liability of Social Workers after *DeShaney*," *Social Work* 38 (January 1993): 64–68; Douglas J. Besharov with Lisa A. Laumann, "Child Abuse Reporting," *Society* 38 (May/June 1996): 40–46; and Douglas J. Besharov, "Why the System Fails Abused Children," *Trial* (March 1997): 18–22.

Several scholarly works have addressed the issues of child abuse and child welfare specifically within the context of the history of family law. These include Michael J. Grossberg, *Governing the Hearth: Law and Family in Nineteenth-Century America* (Chapel Hill: University of North Carolina Press, 1985); Martha Minow, editor, *Family Matters: Readings in Family Lives and the Law* (New York: New Press, 1993); Barbara Bennett Woodhouse, *The Status of Children: A Story of Emerging Rights, Cross-Currents: Family Law in England and the United States* (New York: Oxford University Press, 2000); Dorothy E. Roberts, "Is There Justice in Children's Rights? The Critique of Federal Family Preservation Policy," *University of Pennsylvania Journal of Constitutional Law* 2 (December 1999): 112–140; and Stuart J. Baskin, "State Intrusion into Family Affairs: Justifications and Limitations," *Stanford Law Review* 26 (June 1974): 1383–1409. Researchers in this area should also consult the encyclopedic reference volume edited by Robert H. Mnookin and D. Kelly Weisberg, *Child, Family, and State: Problems and Materials on Children and the Law*, 4th ed. (Gaithersburg, NY: Aspen, 2000).

Numerous scholars have examined the Supreme Court's opinion in *DeShaney v. Winnebago County* within this context. Those I found the most helpful to my own understanding include Martha Minow, "Words and the Door to the Land of Change: Law, Language, and Family Violence," *Vanderbilt Law Review* 43 (November 1990): 1665–1699; Barbara Bennett Woodhouse, "'Who Owns the Child?': *Meyer* and *Pierce* and the Child as Property,"

William and Mary Law Review 33 (Summer 1992): 995–1122; and Catherine A. Crosby-Currie and N. Dickon Reppucci, "The Missing Child in Child Protection: The Constitutional Context of Child Maltreatment from *Meyer* to *DeShaney*," *Law and Policy* 21 (April 1999): 129–159. Three foundational legal opinions in modern U.S. family law are *O' Connell v. Robert Turner*, 55 Ill. 280 (1870); *Meyer v. Nebraska*, 262 U.S. 390 (1923); and *Pierce v. Society of Sisters*, 268 U.S. 510 (1925).

In the months following the Court's rendering of the *DeShaney* opinion legal scholarship abounded, virtually all of it critical of the decision. Although I read numerous law review articles, I found the following to be representative of a range of legal arguments scholars presented in their critiques of the Court. These were Laurence Tribe, "Revisiting the Law," *New York University Law Review* 64 (June 1989): 726–731 and "The Curvature of Constitutional Space: What Lawyers Can Learn from Modern Physics," *Harvard Law Review* 103 (November 1989): 1–38; Laura Oren, "The State's Failure to Protect Children and Substantive Due Process: *DeShaney* in Context," *North Carolina Law Review* 68 (April 1990): 659–731; Susan Bandes, "The Negative Constitution: A Critique," *Michigan Law Review* 88 (August 1990): 2271–2347; and Akhil Reed Amar and Daniel Widawsky, "Commentary: Child Abuse as Slavery: A Thirteenth Amendment Response to *DeShaney*," *Harvard Law Review* 105 (April 1992): 1359–1385. Curry First offered his own assessment in "'Poor Joshua!': The State's Responsibility to Protect Children from Abuse," *Clearinghouse Review* (August/September 1989): 525–534. The *American Bar Association Journal* also covered the case in 1988 and 1989.

Print coverage during the months preceding and after the *DeShaney* opinion was handed down in February 1989 was extensive. Local and regional newspapers I researched were the Appleton *Post-Crescent*, the Oshkosh *Northwestern*, the *Milwaukee Journal* (available on microfilm at the Wisconsin Historical Society in Madison), and the *Chicago Tribune*. National coverage I examined included *Time* (March 6, 1989): 56 and the *Los Angeles Times*, *St. Louis Post-Dispatch*, *USA Today*, and the *Boston Globe*. The most thorough discussions of the case and its larger ramifications, however, can be found in the *New York Times*, particularly in a series of well-informed pieces by Linda Greenhouse.

Board of Regents v. Roth (1972), 111, 112, 118, 119, 120, 123
Boddie v. Connecticut (1971), 139
Bodily security, 92
  protections for, 88, 89, 118
Bodnar, John, 18, 20, 21, 36
Bono, David A., 113
Boston Globe, DeShaney ruling and, 137
"Botched rescue attempt" model, 106
Bowers, Timothy L., 29, 30, 95
Bowers v. DeVito (1982), 93, 100, 130
Brace, Charles Loring, street children and, 44
Brennan, William J., 105, 108, 113
  dissent by, 12, 127–129, 130–131, 132
  Joshua's entitlements and, 119–120
  Sullivan and, 118
Bright line standard, 93, 122
Brophy, Thomas A., 134
Brownmiller, Susan, 67
Brown v. Board of Education (1954), 144
Buck v. Bell (1927), 87–88

CAPTA. See Congress of the Child Abuse and Treatment Act
Cardozo, Benjamin, 85, 87
Carter, Jimmy, 67, 113, 145
Carver, Judge, 77
Caseworkers, 49, 55
  as intermediaries, 7
  intervention by, 60
  judgment by, 8
  life of typical, 50–51
  men as, 51
  petitions by, 56–57
  punitive attitudes of, 88
Central Wisconsin Center for the Developmentally Disabled, 76, 82
CES. See Committee on Economic Security
Charity ladies, 46

Chicago School of Civics and Philanthropy, 50
Chicago Tribune, 142
  on lawsuits/liability, 134–135
Child abuse
  causes/nature of, 9
  criminal prosecution for, 55
  detecting, 56, 59
  diagnosing, 29
  Fourteenth Amendment and, 8
  ignored, 114
  increase in, 59, 66
  intervention in, 116
  investigation of, 66, 122–123
  issue of, 1, 3, 10, 11, 15, 40, 52–53
  legislation, 57
  media and, 2, 61
  new forms of, 54
  overreporting of, 143
  parental rights and, 141
  pediatric awakening to, 56
  preventing, 46, 56, 59, 67, 88, 103, 113, 114, 145
  public interest in, 61, 68, 138
  resolution of, 23, 113
  suspected, 7, 114, 143
  technology and, 66
Child Abuse and Treatment Act (1974), 145
Child Abuse Legislation in the 1970s (American Humane Association), 55
Child abusers, historical constants among, 53–54
  public outrage at, 59
Child development, 22, 23, 24
Childhood/infant mortality, reducing, 46
Child labor, 6, 40
Child protection, 12, 21, 57, 123
  laws, 18, 56, 145
  "medicalization" of, 53
  movement, 41, 131
  private/public realm in, 61
  state responsibility for, 24
  system, 7, 18, 20, 29, 40, 64
  Victorian model of, 45

Child protection services, 4, 11, 56, 87, 111, 131, 140
    Kemmeter and, 22
    regulation of, 57
Child protection workers, 7, 23, 27, 32, 43, 55, 58, 73, 111, 114
    alcoholism and, 41
    negligence and, 108
    police opinions and, 20
    training for, 74, 135
    women as, 44
Children, free agents and, 139
    needs/interests of, 5
    out of wedlock, 48
    protections for, 7, 99–100
    removing, 8, 20, 41, 44, 58, 85, 115, 118, 121, 133
    rights of, 5, 44, 93, 118, 144
    vulnerability of, 139
    See also Abused children
Children's liberation, 4–5, 68
Children's Rights Project (ACLU), 109, 110, 142
Child savers, 41, 74
    poor families and, 42
    social control and, 42
Child welfare, 7, 27, 40, 46, 47, 53
    ascendant medical/ psychological model of, 55
    system, 128–129
Child welfare agencies, 6–7, 87
    family units and, 145
    priorities of, 116
    protection from, 109
Child Welfare League of America, 55
City of New Kensington, suit against, 142
Civil lawsuits, 40, 87, 100
    summary judgment and, 97
Civil rights, 44, 58–59, 68
    expansion of, 4, 101
    individuals and, 5
    scope of, 139
Civil rights law, 4, 9–10, 89, 108, 109
    child abuse and, 68

DeShaney case and, 12
    federal, 96
Clinton, Bill, 113
Coffey, John L., 103
Committee on Economic Security (CES), 52
Congress of the Child Abuse and Treatment Act (CAPTA), 56
Costin, Lela B., 58
Council of State Governments, amicus brief by, 116
Cover, Robert M., 131
Coverture, 88
Custody, 1, 16–17, 21, 22, 36–37, 38, 43, 57, 64, 76, 82, 83, 109
    DeShaney, Randy and, 14, 15, 86, 141, 145
    as legal concept, 141
    safety and, 121
    seeking, 122, 123
    voluntary surrender of, 45
Cycle of violence, 53–54

Daniels v. Williams, 98, 101, 102, 108, 119
Davidson v. Cannon, 98, 100, 102, 118, 130
    negligence and, 108
    Section 1983 and, 99
Davis, Ruth, 30, 31, 32
DeLacy, Rena, 90
Department of Health and Human Services, 39
Department of Health, Education, and Welfare: Children's Bureau and, 53
Department of Labor, Children's Bureau and, 46
Derozier, Donald, 18, 19, 22
DeShaney, Christine, 25
    custody for, 14, 15
    divorce for, 15
DeShaney, Joshua Eli
    abuse of, 1, 11, 33, 44, 74–75, 115
    behavior of, 26, 31, 32, 72
    birth of, 13, 145